The Singer's Ego

Finding Balance between Music and Life

The Singer's Ego
Finding Balance between Music and Life

*A Guide for Singers and Those Who Teach
and Work with Singers*

Lynn Eustis

GIA Publications, Inc.

Chicago

G–6528
© 2005 GIA Publications, Inc.
7404 S. Mason Ave., Chicago, IL 60638
www.giamusic.com
ISBN: 1-57999-526-8
Cover design: Nikki Wilkens
Book layout: Todd Petersen

Printed in the United States of America

Poets to come! orators, singers, musicians to come!
Not to-day is to justify me and answer what I am for,
But you, a new brood, native athletic, continental, greater than before known,
Arouse! for you must justify me.

I myself but write one or two indicative words for the future,
I but advance a moment only to wheel and hurry back in the darkness.

I am a man who, sauntering along without fully stopping,
turns a casual look upon you and then averts his face,
Leaving it to you to prove and define it,
Expecting the main things from you.

Walt Whitman, *Leaves of Grass*

TABLE OF CONTENTS

Foreword

James Jordan
Westminster Choir College

What is the popular conception of the artist? Gather a thousand descriptions, and the resulting composite is the portrait of a moron: he is held to be childish, irresponsible, and ignorant or stupid in everyday affairs.

The picture does not necessarily involve censure or unkindness. These deficiencies are attributed to the intensity of the artist's pre-occupation with his particular kind of fantasy and to the unworldly nature of the fantastic itself. The bantering tolerance granted to the absentminded professor is extended to the artist. Biographers contrast the artlessness of his judgments with the high attainment of his art, and while his naïveté or rascality are gossiped about, they are viewed as signs of Simplicity and Inspiration which are handmaidens of Art. And if the artist is inarticulate and lacking in the usual repositories of fact and information, how fortunate, it is said, that nature contrived to divert him from all worldly distractions so that he may be single-minded in regards to his special office.

– Mark Rothko, *The Artist's Reality*, p. 1

Several months ago, I received a book manuscript from former student and friend Lynn Eustis. I must admit that I rolled my eyes and chuckled a bit when I read the title: *The Singer's Ego*. While I thought she might have something to say, I was not prepared for what she put forward in the book.

Having written two books on what I believe are components of the musician's inner journey and having recently birthed a third such book entitled *The Musician's Walk*, I naively believed that I was aware of all perspectives of the "inner life" of a musician. I also believed that after almost thirty years in the choral conducting profession I truly have begun to understand the psyche of the ensemble, that I understood "how they work."

Well, as I read Dr. Eustis' book, I became acutely aware of my shortcomings or, rather, my blindness to the emotional complexities of singers. Because of her book, I approach the singers in my ensembles differently. I am sorry to say that I never thought about the inner confusion singers face when they are unable to separate their voice from their "human" self. That is, when the voice isn't working well, singers sometimes find it hard to realize that this is not a reflection upon them as human beings, but simply means that the voice didn't work that day. I also never contemplated the effects of *my* words and body language upon the vocal and emotional health of my singers. And I never used such empathy to help singers distinguish and separate, when necessary, less than stellar singing with their soulful existence as people.

This book is extremely provocative, innovative, and, if I may say so, brave. Dr. Eustis uses her own "walk" to try to draw insights into the singer's life. While the book is entertaining at times, its bittersweet message is one that needs to be heeded by anyone who works with singers, especially conductors and coaches. Artists in general and singers, specifically, are fragile not because of some genetic mutation known only to artists but are vulnerable because their instrument is their body. Philosophers and psychologists have explored the mind/body dualism from Descartes onward. However, the music profession in general and music education in specific have not faced the profound psychological issues confronting singers that inherently cohabitate the consciousness and unconsciousness of the singer.

After reading the manuscript, I started the year with my new ensemble at Westminster Choir College, the Westminster Williamson Voices, with a slightly different mindset. I am convinced that my newfound awareness of the "singer's condition" and "psyche" has further transformed my teaching and my rehearsals. I approach correction in rehearsals in other ways than I did in the past. I am conscious, now, of the impact of my words and actions on the singers.

I have known Dr. Eustis for the better part of my teaching career, and she student taught with me at Lewisburg High School in Lewisburg, Pennsylvania. What gives this book the strongest credibility is that it is written from the inside out by a gifted artist and singer. It is remarkable to me that despite her abundant musical gifts and training at the Curtis Institute, that the major obstacles to her musical world were not musical, but her struggle to balance the human situation and the singing instrument.

This is a great book, and everyone who teaches or works with singers in any capacity should be required to read it. Based on my experience, it will transform the way you work with singers, and, more important, allow for their musical growth through a deeper understanding of the singer's self.

One of teaching's great rewards is when your students become your teacher, which lets you know that in some small way you have had a positive effect on them. The highest compliment I can give to this book is that I have learned and have grown tremendously by reading it.

I encourage you to read and experience this brave journey into the inner world of the singer.

Acknowledgements

Neither this book nor my life as a teacher would have materialized without two wonderful people: my parents, Richard and Carole Eustis. They taught me to treat everyone, especially students, as equal human beings worthy of love and respect. I thank them for a life and home filled with books, music, conversation, laughter, and a constant stream of students and teachers of all ages. My brother, John, and my sister, Jessica, are lifelines for me, along with their spouses, Beth and Strider, respectively. Their children, my nephews Thomas, Noah, and Jake, make life beautiful every day.

I could not have written this without the support and mentoring of Warren Henry, William Payn, Todd Wilson, Robert Hay, Michael McConnell, and James Scott.

Special thanks must go to James Jordan for believing in me from the very beginning. His courageous, soulful works inspired this project.

To my wonderful teachers (not already mentioned above) in chronological order: Barbara Castiglia, Elsie Shulman, Grace Boyce, Benton Stark, Jim David, Dwight Peltzer, Jackson and Martha Hill, William Duckworth, Lois Svard, Jay Pierson, Ellen Faull, Mikael Eliasen, Danielle Orlando, Joanna Levy, Yvonne Ciannella, Douglas Fisher, Roy Delp, Jeffrey Kite-Powell, and Douglass Seaton.

Many thanks to the people at the Green House in Denton, Texas, especially Andy, Nat, Natalie, Megan, Matt, Nicole, Desiree, Alicia, Jolie, and Kenny, for providing me with a friendly, welcoming place to write.

My students have contributed more than I can say to my ideas about what we do. I am proud to learn from them each and every day. I must offer special thanks to the students in my studio at the University of North Texas who read sections of the book and generously shared their ideas and experiences since the project began in summer 2002. This exceptional group also saw me through some very difficult personal times. When my father passed away, they brought flowers to my office every Monday morning for the rest of the semester. I thank you from the bottom of my heart for all that you have meant to me: Colin Ashley, Emily Bailey, Rebecca Choate Beasley, Jenny Beckman, Charlotte Chambers, Sarah Nelson Craft, Riki Darding, Nancy Davis, Rebecca Duren, Nilda Melida Gomez, Jennifer Harvey, Leah Jenkins, Sibyl Kirkpatrick-McKee, Marissa Luciani, Brian Nedvin, Dianna Perry, Lynne Rutherford, AnnMarie Sandy, Brian Shadowens, Matthew Vala, Jennifer Wallace, and Summer Lee Yancey. This book is my gift from you and for you, and my welcome to all of the students I will come to know in the future.

The Singer's Ego

Chapter One: Introduction— How Are Singers Different?

When I told people I was writing about the singer's ego, without fail they chuckled and commented about what a long book it would be. Some said that the terms are redundant; if you are a singer, you have an ego. Anyone who personally knows a singer laughs because he understands how complicated his or her emotional life can be. One teacher I studied with in New York kept a sign on her piano stand that read "Crisis in Progress." Most people who seek out the spotlight are understood to have different ego needs than the rest of the population. A strong sense of ego is a necessity in order to be a successful performing artist. Singers, however, are uniquely affected by issues of confidence and ego development for a wide variety of reasons.

Though opera singers are generally considered to be larger than life, thanks to Bugs Bunny, Luciano Pavarotti, and others, the phrase "It ain't over until the fat lady sings" carries a loaded meaning for those of us who live and work in the field. Ask a classical instrumentalist about singers, and you will hear a long parade of jokes about singers' egos, their limited capacities to read music (here we sopranos and tenors are special targets), and their various other foibles, all of which imply that singers are a different breed. The operatic ego (translation, "oversized") may develop in part as a defense mechanism against these slurs. We have all heard stories about opera *divas* and *divos* and their incredible acts of egotism. Yet professional athletes behave this way in front of television cameras

3

virtually every day, as do Hollywood actors and actresses, all of whom are paid considerably more than the average opera singer.

The term *diva* has become so widely accepted into our language that my computer's spell-check stopped on the word *divo* but not *diva*, both of which are Italian words. Pop culture now uses the word *diva* to describe superstars such as Mariah Carey and Whitney Houston. Classical sopranos have resorted increasingly to *prima donna*, which in Italian means "first woman." While this phrase actually refers to the leading lady of the opera, it has come to have a negative connotation, particularly in its borrowed "English" form. Interestingly, no equivalent term exists for the male gender. (Perhaps further discussion is necessary on why a woman leading the cast merits a special designation but a man doesn't.)

Stars in any field can suffer from overblown egos, and musicians are no exception. Singers do behave in ways that often confound other musicians, our families, and our friends. My quest to define the singer's ego began in self-defense during arguments with other musicians. I could not deny that singers seem to have particular difficulties managing their insecurities. As a singer and a teacher of singers, I know that there are legitimate reasons for our struggle. I began writing them down simply to organize my ideas on the subject.

The Instrument Is You

Psychologically speaking, there is something particularly naked about actually being your own instrument. No other musician deals with this exact situation. I find it interesting that pianists tend to argue more vehemently than any other instrumentalists that singers have "no excuse" for their behavior. I believe it is because pianists are the only musicians who do not perform exclusively on their own instruments. Most other musicians travel with their own instruments. If the instrument malfunctions, the musician may have it repaired or, if necessary, replaced. Pianists must learn the intricacies of a new instrument in every concert venue, often with limited rehearsal time. In both cases, however, the instrument is external to the person using it, and its tonal characteristics are not considered synonymous with the musician himself.

Many singers deal with the problem of separating themselves from "the voice." Dozens of singers I know will describe the actions of "the voice" as completely alien to their own desires, as though "the voice" itself were another person misbehaving in their relationship in an attempt to force separation. The blurred line between the voice and the true self leads to enormous highs and lows. When the instrument is you and your performance receives thunderous applause, the high is tremendous. The "off" nights, on the other hand, can't simply be left onstage. One student told me she holds back when she sings because of her fear that if someone doesn't like the sound of her voice, she "can't go out and buy a new one." If she doesn't allow the true sound of her voice to be heard, I reminded her, she will not receive encouragement from others, and she will trap herself in a chicken-versus-egg conundrum.

The lows of musical criticism are even more devastating when the singer is unable to see other means of self-validation. "If you could never sing another note after today, you would be a wonderful person with a full life," I might say to a disbelieving student. Typically this comment follows a lengthy discussion about how terrible the student feels because her voice isn't working, proof that she will never be able to accomplish anything. My statement seems natural to me after my own journey through life, but the student is generally resistant to the idea. If I press the issue and add that I think she doesn't know she is a great and interesting person completely independent of her singing voice, the tears flow, and the student says, "How did you know I felt that way?"

Social Issues

I was twenty-five years old when I faced a surprising dilemma: somewhere along the line, I had confused my voice with my true self. Like many young singers, I had become accustomed to receiving a great deal of attention for my singing. I had the added burden of being an awkward, slightly overweight, shy child, particularly as I entered my high school years. Throughout my early childhood, I was the nerd who knew how to read when I started kindergarten. This ability helped me socially up to a certain point, the point at which the other children were expected to know how to read as well, and I became the person who threw off the curve.

I still remember the first time my voice brought me social acceptance. I was thirteen years old, and I was auditioning for summer theatre at the high school where I would soon begin my freshman year. The show was *Man of La Mancha*, and I was up for the part of Don Quixote's niece, Antonia. I sang her song, "I'm Only Thinking of Him," with the microphone in one hand and the book in the other because I had unknowingly prepared a different piece. When the cast list went up and my name was on the part, one of only eight principals in a cast of about sixty students, my life changed. Suddenly I was accepted by the popular older kids in the group, simply because I could sing. From that day forward, I began to pull out of the adolescent mire and blossom into something much more special than I had been thus far, at least in my eyes. For better for worse, my ego became even more securely tied to my vocal ability.

My newfound confidence initially manifested itself in mostly positive ways. I continued to get roles in high school (sometimes losing friends along the way—see Chapter Seven). I went on to major in music at Bucknell University, where the Chapel Choir served as my social group. To my surprise (and my teacher's unabashed shock), I was accepted to study at the Curtis Institute of Music in the master of music degree program in opera. Because I was one of the youngest singers in the program, some of the older singers took maternal roles with me. All of the effects my talents had on my life to this point were positive, until I encountered the most serious vocal problems of my career. These problems forced me to confront my belief that my voice was my entire identity. (See Chapter Four.)

In my teaching, I have seen many cases with similar trajectories. The student experiences great success, both socially and musically, throughout the high school years. This social network is the very reason many of these students decide to major in music in college. At some point during undergraduate study, the student faces a crisis when he or she fails to grow in one area or the other. Sometimes the problem is not getting the role or the solo for the first time, losing it to an older student or to a more qualified student at the same level. This can be devastating when it happens for the first time at such a late age. Sometimes the crisis is related to vocal health; the student may be reaching the age when he or she can no longer stay out all night and sing well the next day. This problem is especially trying when the student is experiencing social success but not the expected musical success upon entering college. Whatever the nature of the crisis, the student is faced with a loss of self when the voice is taken out of the equation. A healthy student with an ego built on the total self will deal with these problems more effectively.

One of my students at Florida State University, where I served as a teaching assistant, entered the program in a state of crisis. Karen* was angry that she had not been accepted into the performance degree program and that she had to study with a teaching assistant instead of with a faculty member. I dealt with her as gingerly as I could until several weeks went by and she failed to learn any of her pieces with any acceptable degree of accuracy. I sent the pianist away and asked Karen what she needed from me; if she needed simpler repertoire, that was certainly an option. Karen told me she was tired of singing; she'd been singing since she was five, and she was just sick of it. I told her about the time I announced to Ellen Faull (my Curtis voice teacher) that I didn't want to sing anymore. (Ellen Faull was on the Juilliard faculty, but Curtis allowed us to study with any teacher as long as the administration approved our choice.) I gave Karen the same advice I'd been given: Don't sing for a full week, not in the car, not in the shower, not one note, not even if you want to, and I guarantee you will want to before the week is out.

Karen reacted exactly as I had years before: "There's no way I'm going to want to sing. I hate it, and I'm through." I attempted to replicate Miss Faull's wise smile. The following week Karen was ready to have a lesson again, albeit still a bit reluctantly. Gradually,

* Names have been changed throughout for anonymity.

she made friends at Florida State and learned to trust both herself and me. She went on to win third place in Freshmen Women at the Regional NATS Auditions and to win the role of Cissy in the Florida State University Opera's production of *Albert Herring* that spring. She passed her next audition for the performance degree program with flying colors. Unfortunately, Karen had a heart condition that forced her to leave school after that triumphant year.

It has been my personal experience thus far in my teaching career that female singers tend to be more likely than males to equate their feelings of identity with their voices. Women are more deeply devastated when their voices malfunction, and they are more prone to the depression that may prevent them from taking corrective action. The positive side of this tendency, however, is that women will more readily invest themselves emotionally when they sing. Conversely, male singers don't tend to identify themselves so completely through their vocal abilities. When I offer a suggestion in the studio, I can sometimes sense my female students thinking (or in some cases, saying), "You think I'm terrible, I am terrible, I've always been terrible, I'll never make it, etc." A male student in the same situation will more often reply, "You're right, that wasn't good. Let me try it again." They avoid the trap of self-deprecation and move directly to the correction. Male singers are susceptible to posturing rather than allowing their true emotions to be seen and heard, however, and they may have more difficulty achieving vocal and musical freedom. Exceptions abound on both sides of these broad generalizations and the most successful students of either gender are the ones who can both express their emotions freely and handle criticism by moving forward to address the problem.

For students with special gifts, musical success may come at the expense of social success. If the student is the only freshman accepted into the upper-level choir, for example, or wins a solo role over more advanced students, the student suddenly may be cast out of the social group. Perhaps the student is readily accepted by the older students but still finds it difficult to fit in with peers of different ages. The successful singer will always be scrutinized by the others in the group to a greater extent than those who avoid standing out in any way. Not all singers can handle the increased social pressure of this role, and withdrawal may seem to be the easiest solution. This withdrawal allows the other singers to characterize the "star" as aloof or snobbish and ostracize him or her further without guilt. These complex relations can be very difficult for young singers to negotiate, and they all contribute to confusion about the vocal ego.

Physiology and Discipline

Lack of control over the physiology of the instrument causes singers of all ages much worry. All performers suffer from diminished capacity when they are ill, but every element of the singer's sound can be affected by an illness within the instrument itself. Singers generally perform from memory, a skill that is compromised by many conditions. When the singer's voice malfunctions in public, the singer may be devastated by the effect, real or imagined, of the failure on their career. The decision whether to sing when one is ill can be agonizing, particularly if the performance represents a pivotal career step. All of this pressure often results in hypervigilance regarding the state of one's health. Other professional musicians frequently joke about singers who seem to be hypochondriacs. Not surprisingly, many singers have family and friends in their lives who brand them as "selfish" because of their devotion to physical health. My own family members have occasionally characterized me as selfish but then explained away my behavior by attributing it to my career. This lack of understanding can be very hurtful to a singer, whether or not it is intended as such.

Many full-time professional singers complain about the discipline of staying in good physical health. Singers carry their instruments with them wherever they go, and thus they use the instruments for a wide variety of other purposes in the course of a normal day. The average non-singer probably doesn't think twice about going to a football game or a loud dance club, or taking a telemarketing job, yet these activities all present possible dangers for singers. One summer

I developed an ear infection about two months prior to my first *Lucia di Lammermoor* performance. My voice teacher berated me for going swimming at my apartment complex, saying, "You're in training! What were you thinking using a public pool?" Ballet dancers and athletes can relate to this constant pressure, but most non-singing musicians find this level of discipline obsessive.

I personally found it difficult to carry the stress about my physical health with me every day, which is one of the many reasons I chose my present career in academia. Between worrying about the state of my career, about money (constantly), and about every little scratch of the throat, I was becoming a champion neurotic. These days I sing professionally quite a bit, but there are many blessed times in my life when I don't have a performance within a week's time. Occasionally I find the engagements snowballing, and I exceed my comfort level. I hear myself complaining to friends that I'm singing too much, and I smile as I remember my student days when I worried that I wouldn't be singing enough of the time as an adult.

The neurosis about physical health stays with most singers to varying degrees throughout their careers. Recently I had to cancel a performance of Bach's Cantata no. 51, "Jauchzet Gott in allen Landen," the first time in about five years that I had been forced to cancel due to illness. I had caught a bad cold from a student, and I could barely talk, through no fault of my own. The piece was too difficult and the venue (the Boston Early Music Festival) was too important for me to risk performing with a compromised instrument. I cried afterward, and I was terribly upset until the conductor, Lyle Nordstrom, put things back into perspective for me. Nobody had died; I was just unable to sing one day because I had gotten sick. An incident like that one keeps me humble and in tune with what my students are experiencing for the first time.

Text and Its Emotional Implications

Communication is both the most wonderful and the most difficult thing about being a singer. Singers must face the audience without any barriers, expressing specific emotions relative to the text of the material. The texts provide clear ideas about the composer's intentions, for which instrumentalists envy us. But texts also force us to articulate our deepest, most personal emotions without offering the option of anonymity. For example, many songs deal with the subjects of love and sexuality. How many of us would feel completely comfortable showing an entire audience the selves we share with our lovers?

Many singers choose not to reveal much of themselves onstage, offering instead what they think a real person might look like feeling those emotions, or simply choosing not to show any emotion at all. The singers who choose one of these paths, however, rarely become true artists. Some of the most expressive singers I know create barriers around themselves in their daily lives to compensate for the exposure they feel when they perform. Their families and friends are often stunned when they see how completely their shy, reserved singer seems to embody the text in performances. Oddly enough, the opposite is often true as well. A singer who lights up the room in real life often joins the living dead when he or she begins to sing.

The direct nature of the communication of text frightens many singers into non-performance music fields. Singing religious texts in a choir of sixty voices is a very different experience from singing Debussy's "C'est l'extase" from *Ariettes Oubliées* as a soloist, a poem about the moments following a sexual encounter. These are extreme examples, of course, but they illustrate the point: text makes vocal music more explicit in emotional meaning than instrumental music. Even when instrumentalists play sensual music, they are able to "hide" behind the music stand. They never have to face the audience directly and embody the sensual experience.

Texts cover a wide range of subjects, not only love and sex, and singers have to find both composers and texts complementary to their personalities. It can be all too easy for singers to focus on technical aspects of singing and refuse to truly deal with text until much later in their careers. I maintain that all singing is easier and more natural when it begins with the text and its meaning. Small children sing without our encouragement, and their singing is clear and natural until adults begin to "refine" it. It takes some singers many years to rediscover that kind of spontaneity.

Family Attitudes

Family attitudes play an enormous role in the ongoing development of confidence in the singer in the way they shape the singer's thinking and relationships in later life. Many families have no frame of reference for a classical music career. Students who come from educated, artistic families may be more likely to take their studies (and themselves) more seriously than those who do not. If one or both parents are celebrities in the classical music field, the pressure to rebel and choose one's own path can be greater than usual. One accomplished violinist I knew during my student days at Curtis refused to play her instrument after graduation. After some time had passed, her father, a well-known concert pianist, cut her off financially and told her to support herself by playing concerts, which she then did. These days, they frequently perform together. Classical performers may grow up in families of a less artistic nature as well, empowered to follow their dreams by what their families gave them as human beings. Socialization during one's youth is critical to the musician's life, whatever the environment ultimately offers.

I descend from a long line of teachers, so education has always been very important in my life. My great-grandmother was a concert pianist until she gave up her career to get married, an either/or proposition for women in those days. My grandfather John on my father's side was an art teacher for many years at a public high school in New York City, where Maurice Sendak was his most renowned pupil.[1] His wife, my grandmother Dorothy, taught elementary school. As a teenager, she had her own radio show called "Ukelele Dot," at least until her parents heard the show and grounded her. My father's sister Linda is a singer as well as a retired elementary school art teacher.

My parents shaped most of my first thoughts about teachers and their values. My father, Richard, taught English at my public high school, which would have been a nightmare if he hadn't been one of the "cool" teachers. Every semester he would ask his department chair for all of the least advanced classes in exchange for one honors class. He was one of the only teachers who treated these less-advanced students as human beings. After teaching in the slums of Brooklyn, my father was not afraid of these primarily middle class students and their relatively tame modes of misbehaving. My father would always say that he didn't want to teach the mediocre masses; he wanted to work with students at both ends of the spectrum. One of the worst things you could be in our home was average, especially if you were average because you hadn't given the endeavor your best effort.

My mother, Carole, taught kindergarten at a private school on Long Island in the affluent suburb of Roslyn. Most of her students were wealthy, and although our family wasn't, I learned early on that money doesn't necessarily solve anything. Many of these students had everything they could ever want, but that did not protect them from the usual family problems. These children seemed to have far less time with their parents than we did, for one thing. I heard conversations between my parents virtually every day involving particular students and how they could help them through each problematic situation. I learned that it was vital and natural to care about one's students as individuals first, and only second as students of a particular subject.

I was also fortunate enough to have grown up with my grandfather (on my mother's side) who lived with us from the time I was about nine until he passed away in 1993. Most of our friends called him Grandpa, too, and some of my parents' friends called him Big Mike. Grandpa worked for the telephone company, but he loved to draw, especially cartoons. During World War II, his task with the Air Force was to paint voluptuous women on the sides of aircraft to distract the enemy pilots. For years he sent me flowers on my birthday and on Valentine's Day. Grandpa provided a distinct, quiet kind of support for me. He said very little, but he always let me know he believed I was beautiful and special. From him, I learned that we can show our faith in someone we love in many ways other than through verbal declarations.

At present, my immediate family is still heavily involved in education. Until a few months before he passed away, my father was an adjunct professor of English at Penn Technical College. My mother currently evaluates teachers for the United States Federal Government and teaches as a substitute in Pennsylvania elementary schools. My younger sister, Jessica, is an elementary school guidance counselor (she holds a bachelor of arts degree in sociology and a master of arts degree in education, both from Bucknell University). Jessica put herself through her masters program as a single mom, although she has since remarried. My brother, John, pursued a career in the corporate world, and he is presently director of purchasing for Hinckley Yachts, based in Maine. He holds a master of science degree in engineering and a master of business administration degree from the Massachusetts Institute of Technology, both of which he completed in just two years time.

Although I am the only professional singer in my family, we all sang around the piano growing up. My sister and brother were just as involved in musical theater and ensemble singing as I was throughout high school and college. Jessica's voice has a similar quality to mine, although it is a bit lower and duskier, and less formally trained. John is the type of singer for whom karaoke was invented. He has all the confidence in the world, and he sings just well enough to handle the microphone effectively (he can read music, sing in parts, etc., but lacks technique and sophistication of tone). I have often wished to have his sense of abandon when I sing. Recently I spoke with him about it again, and he told me that for him it is less a matter of confidence than of sheer enjoyment in singing because there are no expectations riding on his performance.

In addition to being my first teaching mentor, my father gave me an even more important gift that has shaped and enriched my life: my love of music. I grew up listening to classical music every night at dinner, as well as most of the rest of the time. On Saturday mornings, my mother taught classes at a local community center, and my father would make me listen to such works as *Cavalleria*

Rusticana and *La bohème* while he explained what the singers were saying and why certain lines were important (he did teach literature, after all). When I was a child, there was a popular television program called *Name That Tune*. My dad and I didn't bother much with the show—it was for "lightweights." (My father had a similar Brooklyn term for those who did crossword puzzles with a pencil.) In our living room, we had our own version of the show, one that was much more cutthroat. One of my favorite pastimes was to sit down at the piano while a Mozart piano concerto or something comparable was playing on the stereo and play along with the recording, trying to guess where the piece or the line would go next. I can only imagine what I absorbed about musical form through that activity. One paragraph can hardly begin to summarize the impact that all of my father's encouragement had on my musical life.

In 1994, I sat down with my parents and told them I planned to leave New York City to pursue a doctorate and then a career in academia. In retrospect, I can't fathom why I was nervous about this conversation. My parents were clearly relieved that I was leaving the city and getting a "real job," and overjoyed that I wanted to follow in their career footsteps. I had been the first in my family to complete a masters degree and now I would be the first to complete a doctorate. I had been afraid that my parents would be too invested in the idea of me as an opera singer to accept my new choice. For me, this was the first step toward believing in myself as completely independent of my identity as a singer. This realization greatly improved my performances as a singer. I completed my doctor of music degree in voice performance with an opera emphasis at Florida State University in 1998 and accepted my first position as assistant professor of voice and opera at Howard Payne University for the 1998–99 school year. I have been an assistant professor of voice at the University of North Texas College of Music since fall 1999.

Many of my current students come from very different backgrounds than I had growing up outside of New York City on Long Island. Some of their parents have unrealistic ideas about their child's talents. These parents push their children into careers for which they are ill suited and live vicariously through them. Others have parents who are suspicious about the business of performing, largely because they don't personally know anyone who has taken that path. Most parents want their children to be financially secure, and they are understandably concerned about their child's employment options. A career as an opera singer takes many years to gestate, and some parents would rather see their children married with children before the age of thirty. All of these attitudes affect the singer's ego, particularly as the singer organizes her feelings about singing. At some point, every singer has to decide two things. First, and most important, they have to determine when their life no longer belongs to their parents. The second decision regards singing, which also has to become their own. Singers who pursue it for someone else will never be truly happy or successful.

Beginning to Cope: Vocal Study

The longer I teach, the more convinced I become that ego is critical to any serious vocal pursuit. A good singer possesses many basic skills, including technique, musicianship, language proficiency and communication. If the singer begins a lesson or a performance with a self-critical mindset or confusion about his or her vocal identity, however, the activity is doomed to mediocrity at best. Any adult human being will be susceptible to professional difficulties when his or her sense of self apart from work is not clearly defined. For singers, this clear sense of self is imperative to handle the psychological demands of a performance career.

The word "ego" alone often carries a negative connotation in today's world. The more current term is "self-esteem," which *Merriam-Webster* defines as "confidence and satisfaction in oneself."[2] Without some sense of ego or the self as separate from others, we would have a difficult time negotiating the world. In the professional field of psychology, Raymond J. Corsini and Alan J. Auerbach define the ego ideal as: "the capacity for constructing one's own model... the ideal toward which the person strives or aspires need not be embodied in the environment."[3] We may all agree that this type of ego is desirable, yet we refer to difficult people as having "ego problems" or "big egos" and imply that having an ego at all is a problem.

The *Concise Encyclopedia of Psychology* offers a generally accepted sequence of stages for ego development. In the conscientious stage, achievement is valued "not purely as competitive or social recognition, but measured by the person's own standards." The autonomous stage incorporates a respect and consideration for others as well as oneself. Because people tend to conform to the norms and values of their social groups, singers may have difficulty here as well. If singers tend to act a certain way, they may continue to be competitive and exclude others, i.e., as part of a self-perpetuating pattern of the group as a whole. Teachers can impact students very strongly by creating an environment in the studio or studio class in which the norms are support for the success of others as a way to support their own work as well. At the integrated stage, the person is able to combine concern for both society and the self into one complex thought. The truly artistic singer will need to integrate larger societal concerns into the poetry of the universal human condition that appears in so much of the vocal repertoire.

It may seem that singers are encouraged to ignore all of these later stages of ego development, as they are seen by many as detrimental to developing a competitive edge. This book attempts to address the conflict many singers feel between these warring opinions and to offer ways to compete without losing one's sense of self-respect or basic humanity. I argue that respect for others engenders a fuller acceptance of oneself, which, in turn, enhances one's performance abilities.

In recent years, I have worked with two unusually talented students who have been unable to truly fulfill their early promise, either in an hour or over months and years, despite their unique gifts. These singers started their vocal study far ahead of others in their age group. By junior year, both of them were floundering, barely holding up the average as the other singers surpassed them technically and musically. In both cases, their unrealistic expectations for perfection made it impossible for them to progress as they should have, which further lessened their self-esteem. Did these students suffer from lack of ego or inflated ego? I believe they both lacked *definition* of ego. They weren't sure where their voices ended and they began. I find that this is most often true of the very gifted singers, although I have also seen it in singers on other levels. In both of their cases, the talent level was so high that the rest of the self shrank away in comparison. Both had parents who pushed them to pursue singing, albeit in very different ways. Not only were their lives not their own, but their voices weren't either. While they loved singing, all they could see was the perfection they already should have attained. Eventually they were unable to work at all. Today neither one is singing on a regular basis, which I believe is for the best, and I hope they will find peace in their lives.

Singers who teach voice have an even stronger need for a fully developed ego ideal. The suggestion that many voice teachers are more invested in their own ego needs than in developing the student's confidence is not a new one. When a teacher does not have a solid sense of self apart from the student's accomplishments, it becomes difficult for him or her to remain pure in motive. This lack of integrity has numerous implications for the student's definition of self. The teacher may have trouble choosing appropriate repertoire or allowing the student to grow as an independent artist. It can be tempting to enjoy the adulation of students who are dependent on one's approval and guidance.

For too many of these students, vocal disaster eventually follows, sometimes as early as during the mid-twenties. The inefficient muscle memory may become so deeply embedded that it cannot be successfully reversed. Even if the technical problems can be solved, the student carries emotional baggage from the experience. It is highly traumatic to entrust one's instrument to a teacher and lose all positive reinforcement in the process. These students often apply to graduate schools, hoping to get the basic training they should have received as undergraduates, only to be rejected because they have not demonstrated the requisite technical skills. If they are accepted, these students require the utmost patience and care in the studio.

The older the singer, the more ingrained the muscle memory is, and the phenomenon becomes even more problematic after the age of about twenty-five.

All students begin vocal study with a belief system about singing. At the onset, the system is based purely on ego since the student may know little about technique other than what they do naturally. Some begin with an over-inflated ego, built up by early successes in high school. Over the course of vocal study, the teacher helps the student refine his or her vocal ego, which happens whether or not the teacher is aware of it. Many teachers neglect this aspect of the training, or don't realize its impact on the student's vocal life. If the student is over-invested in his or her vocal talent, or unable to feel a sense of worth without that talent, technical discussion is pointless. The teacher must develop the student's vocal ego, a process that usually begins with belief in both the student's talent and their ability to fix the problems as a team. Sometimes singers who have had bad experiences simply want to find a way to love singing again.

In *Complete Preparation*, Joan Dornemann talks about singers who feel as though they are stuck in a particular situation and cannot change it, no matter how demoralizing it may be for them:

> There's a feeling among young students very often that this is the only voice teacher in the school I want to work with, that only this school has a good opera department...it can result in a lost voice—not a voice lost by illness, but by lack of confidence and self-esteem. Voices are very sensitive to emotional trauma.[4]

Students often feel trapped within a studio or within a program, and they don't understand that they can always make changes if things aren't going well. Loyalty only makes sense if you are still improving and feeling good about your singing. Leaving a teacher and/or a program may be painful, but it can be done compassionately and professionally. You only have one voice and one chance at this career.

Making My Own Choices

When I was a student, I was often told, "If there's something else you want to do, you should do it, because this business is too hard, and there's always someone who wants it more." There is a certain amount of truth in this. If you don't love music enough to need it in your life, you will definitely face an uphill road. On the other hand, if you are not strong enough as a person to believe that you could be fine doing something else, you may go through some difficult times. On tour with the National Opera Company, we used to pass the time on the road by asking each other what our careers would be if we couldn't be singers. A surprising number of singers had no other interests. For me, the question was always easy: I knew I would have gone to law school and most likely would have become a prosecuting attorney. I didn't love the law, though, merely the prospect of law school's intellectual challenge, and I did love teaching. I was desperately unhappy with my career in music, however, until I clarified why I was doing it.

When I decided to discontinue pursuing a full-time career as a singer, I made the decision with the knowledge that I had been performing because other people wanted me to do it for their own reasons. I was living in New York City, working for American Express at the World Financial Center and taking various lessons, coachings, and auditions. Most importantly, I wasn't teaching. Every now and then I would get a nibble on a singing job, and I sang some smaller jobs. More typically, I would be the alternate or the runner-up. I kept receiving just enough reinforcement to keep going.

My teacher sent me out for more acting lessons, this time at Herbert Bergdorf Studios in Greenwich Village, and ordered me not to tell anyone there that I was a singer. I was supposed to sample life without the crutch of my voice. The classes turned out to be a great experience, and I made some encouraging progress as an actor. It was liberating to be in a performance situation without relying on the instant acceptance formerly granted to me because of my vocal ability. Still, my audition results didn't seem to change in any significant way.

When it was time to audition for agents, I found that at this level music was even less important because marketing was the real issue. One agent wanted me to "change everything technically and come back in six months." My teacher wisely told me that I could change teachers and overhaul my technique, but the agent would still have the same objections to me in six months because I just didn't "sell myself." She also told me that I didn't love the spotlight, and I was being stubborn not to want that enough to put my product first. I got very angry until I realized she was right. So many singers enter the profession because they love the applause and the accolades. They care about music, but it takes a distant second to performing anywhere and everywhere. I never wanted it that badly. For me, performances were necessary to have the truly desirable experience of rehearsing and making choices with my colleagues.

I considered the situations in which I felt most at home in my musical life. For several summers I was musical director of the Summer Musical Theater program at Friends Academy, a private high school on Long Island. While I felt comfortable rehearsing the group, it was always the individual coachings I enjoyed most. Recently, we produced the Marvin Hamlisch musical *Smile* based on the 1975 Michael Ritchie film of the same title, a satire of the world of beauty pageants. I fought hard to cast a very shy young woman named Ellen in the important role of the quiet, unsophisticated girl who decides that standing up for her principles is more important than winning the pageant. I worked with Ellen every night before rehearsals to get her singing voice in shape for the role. On opening night, when she sang her final confident lines with beauty and honesty, I felt a deep satisfaction that I had never felt when I sang myself.

I told my family and friends that I was leaving New York to pursue a doctorate in opera at Florida State University, where I had been offered a teaching assistantship. I had talked about leaving long before I did, only to have people tell me I was "too talented" to give it up. My teacher told me it was a good decision, that my voice didn't have to be an albatross hanging around my neck. One of my closest friends said I had "gotten pretty far for someone who didn't want to do this," and I should feel good about that. I had been going through the motions of auditioning for everything and taking all kinds of workshops when I didn't feel the same ambition that others did. With the help of a kind, patient therapist, I slowly figured out that what I really wanted was to teach in the university environment and to pursue my singing as part of that career.

In graduate school and later at the beginning of a full-time performance career, the all-or-nothing nature of singing becomes overwhelming. For most singers, this is the first stage of life in which they dedicate their work entirely to singing, and the stakes become higher than they have ever been. At this point, singers who still have major vocal ego issues are at a serious disadvantage. The voice takes such a large proportion of their energy and time that it can assume too much importance in the singer's sense of self. In addition, most singers are not aware of alternate options for careers (other than headlining at the Met), and the fear of falling short of their goals can be paralyzing. During this time, many singers begin to question their commitment to the profession as well as whether they have the requisite talent to justify pursuing the dream. One of the elements they often ignore is their own temperament and whether they are performers at heart. This stage of the singer's life is arguably the most difficult emotionally and the most critical in terms of career direction. High levels of stress often accompany it, from performance anxiety to concerns about every aspect of life itself.

Entering a career as a professional singer, or as a teacher of singers, is a daunting prospect. The true singer/artist cannot be afraid to delve deeply and to examine all aspects of music, emotion, and relationships with other people. The process begins with a firm knowledge of one's strengths and weaknesses, independent of comparison to others, so that one can enjoy a life in music free of ego distractions. No singer should consider pursuing a career until he or she has explored all of these emotional issues and reached an understanding of his or her own needs and desires. It is too easy to be pressured by others in one direction or another. A career as a musical artist is by definition a personal choice.

I hope that this book and the questions following selected chapters will help you to explore the many experiences in your life and aspects of your emotional life that have come together to make you a singer and/or teacher.

Notes

1. My grandfather is mentioned in Selma Lanes' 1998 book *The Art of Maurice Sendak.*
2. *Merriam-Webster's Collegiate Dictionary* (Springfield, Massachusetts: Merriam-Webster, Inc., 1995).
3. Raymond J. Corsini and Alan J. Auerbach, eds, *Concise Encyclopedia of Psychology, Second Edition* (New York: John Wiley & Sons, 1996).
4. Joan Dornemann, *Complete Preparation* (New York: Excalibur Publishing, 1992), 97.

Further Exploration

1. What is your gut reaction to the word "*diva?*" Do you consider yourself one?

   _____

   _____

   _____

   _____

   Someone calls you a *diva*. Is it a compliment, a judgment, or both?

   _____

   _____

   _____

2. Think of three singers who are "bad *divas*." (1) _____
   They can be famous singers or singers   (2) _____
   you know personally. List three character   (3) _____
   traits that describe them.

   List the traits of "good *divas*."   (1) _____
                                               (2) _____
                                               (3) _____

3. List five positive things about yourself (other than your singing voice).

   (1)_____

   (2) _____

   (3) _____

   (4) _____

   (5) _____

Look carefully at your list. How do these things make you unique? How does each one come into your singing and help you to be yourself when you sing? Think about types of music in which these personal aspects are most valuable.

_____

_____

_____

_____

_____

_____

_____

_____

(Continue on another piece of paper if needed.)

4. Recall a time when you felt socially accepted because of your voice or through your singing activities. Rest in the good feelings you remember.

Recall a time when a friend rejected you because you got a solo (or role, etc.) they wanted for themselves (or vice versa). Consider how that experience changed you.

Have you ever minimized your success to "fit in?"

_____

_____

_____

_____

_____

_____

_____

5. When someone (a teacher, conductor, coach) critiques your singing, how do you react? Do you focus on the task, or do you feel personally rejected? Does it vary from person to person?

_____

_____

_____

_____

_____

What is your primary goal when you attend a voice lesson?

_____

_____

6. When your voice is compromised by illness or fatigue, do you still feel okay with yourself, or does the world seem to be clouded over?

_____

_____

_____

Should you spend more or less effort protecting your voice?

_____

List some healthy behaviors you are currently following to take care of your instrument.

_____

_____

_____

_____

List some unhealthy things you occasionally do to "let off steam."

_____

_____

7. Are you grateful to have text when you sing, or do you wish singing were more instrumental in nature, with no text at all?

_____

_____

Think back to the childhood singing you did just for yourself when no one else was around. Did you make up words? What was (were) your favorite song(s)?

_____

_____

_____

8. Write a history of music in your family going back to your grandparents using the two columns below. It's okay if one of them is empty!

Professional Musicians   *Listening Habits*

_____   _____

_____   _____

_____   _____

_____   _____

a) What kinds of music did you hear at home while you were growing up? If you didn't hear a lot of classical vocal music, you will find it helpful to listen to a great deal of it now, just to expose yourself.

_____

_____

b) With whom in your family or circle of friends do you find the greatest acceptance for your choice of music as a career?

_____

c) If you are a teacher, what is the history of the profession in your family? Who were your most influential role models?

_____

_____

_____

9. Why do you sing? This is a comprehensive and difficult question, so let's break it down. Check any of the answers below that apply to you.

I sing because:

_____ I enjoy the physical sensations of singing.

_____ I have a genuine love for music.

_____ I have always received attention because of my voice.

_____ I have a loud voice.

_____ I have a beautiful voice.

_____ I have come too far to change to something else now.

_____ I want to be onstage, and I love the feeling the applause gives me.

_____ I am better than a lot of the other singers I know.

_____ I enjoy the camaraderie of my vocal activities.

_____ My parents have always wanted me to do it.

_____ My teacher told me that I have a world-class voice.

_____ I want to express myself to other people.

_____ I have a thirst for foreign languages.

_____ I can't imagine doing anything else.

_____ _____

Chapter Two: Confidence vs. Conceit

Understanding the Difference

All singers need confidence in order to perform, particularly in the face of repeated rejection. At what point does confidence become conceit? The dividing line is different for everyone. The initial differentiating factor seems to be based in emotional reality. Healthy confidence grows from knowledge of one's worth, regardless of outer circumstances, while conceit begins with exaggeration of one's abilities, especially in comparison to others. Singers may feel that this exaggerated idea of comparative standing is necessary in order to compensate for their fears, or worse, in order to intimidate other singers as a way of elevating themselves. Too many singers strive to present an image of strength instead of working to build true confidence. Sometimes this attitude comes from the idea that perception is reality, and objective measurement in music is indeed limited.

The lack of objective measurement in the vocal world can be confusing, but it can also be liberating. In the world of athletics, success is typically determined through a point system. Because the competitions begin with an objective standard, such as most touchdowns or fewest technical deductions, the judges have little room for subjective opinion. (Interestingly, figure skating is one of the only Olympic sports that factors in a score for artistry. At the 2002 Olympics, the figure skating competition became a source of controversy when the gold medal was allegedly bought by the Russian team.) In the vocal world, it is just as easy to rationalize that someone else won for the wrong reasons as it is to believe that you won for the right reasons. Furthermore, these subjective results are rarely considered the final word by the business in general. In most professional situations, with the obvious exception of competitions, no one else has to perform badly for another singer to perform well. The ego that is based on exalting oneself at the expense of others is built on a shaky foundation easily crumbled by outside events.

There are practical as well as emotional and moral reasons to believe in one's talents without needing to make others inferior first. In the professional world, no one wants to work with someone who is unpleasant and disdainful of others. In many cases, mediocre singers are hired back every season simply because they are easy to work with for three weeks, or seven weeks, or whatever the season's term. The flip side, however, is that the numbers are too small for bad behavior at one company to go unnoticed by most of the others. The word catches like wildfire, and soon the offending singer can barely find work in the chorus.

Many young singers think that they are the exception to the rule, that their world-class voices exempt them from having to be courteous. Unfortunately, some of them take their cue from teachers who tell them that acknowledging anyone else's talent would somehow lessen their own accomplishments. In today's world, virtually no singer can survive this ungracious behavior over the long term. Several internationally renowned singers have recently been barred from certain major opera houses for *diva* tantrums, despite their arguably unparalleled talents. We can be sure that the climate has changed for the new millennium when the Juilliard School, always on the cutting edge, discusses instituting a new course entitled "Spirituality and the Professional Musician." The days of tyrannical conductors and impossible *divas* appear to be over in these politically correct times. Singers who want to avoid these labels have to find ways to believe in themselves without either being unrealistic about their abilities or taking a bully's approach to competition.

James Jordan writes of the importance of spiritual and emotional centering in his book *The Musician's Soul*.[1] Teachers and conductors (and to a large degree, individual performers) go through a series of emotions when the students are not improving as we would like. We have a split second to determine how we will react in these situations. Because of our perfectionism we often become angry, and we turn that anger back at the students, which is a form of "scape-goating." We can, however, decide to approach the situation from the standpoint of acceptance, both of self and of the students, and help the students to find another way. If we have not learned to accept ourselves and to accept our mistakes, Jordan says, we will be ineffective as musicians. We will approach each musical event with a sense of masquerading as we try to hide our fallibility from ourselves as well as the group.[2]

Our envy of others is often what drives us to hide our imperfections. According to Jordan, musicians envy "the perfect sound" in general, and then others' musical skills, artistry, creative spirits, and technical skills.[3] True artists are most deeply motivated by the search for the elusive perfect sound. We hear another soprano sing beautifully, and we acknowledge the sound's beauty even while part of our heart burns with envy, knowing we will never sound exactly like that. As artists, we must focus on the wonder of what is possible when we hear beautiful sounds made by others. These sounds do not make us any less unique or any less capable of making a sound no other person can create. The music made by others serves as an example for us, to inspire us to make sounds illuminated by our individual selves.

Most musicians play in ways that reflect their personalities. A quiet, introverted flautist may play conservatively though beautifully, while a showboat pianist may excel in flashy Romantic works. To some degree, our temperaments lead us to particular instruments from the beginning. Most of the trumpeters I have known have been confident, charismatic people, for example. I have spoken with many pianists who gave up attempting solo careers in part because they didn't want to spend their lives alone in the practice room. The sheer difficulty of establishing a solo piano career steers away many less independent souls as well. By comparison, singers are often extroverted, animated people who are highly sensitive to the opinions of others.

Singers may be more sensitive than other musicians because they are more personally exposed. For one thing, our budding voices are more likely to become apparent earlier than are any potential affinities for an instrument. We are all exposed to public singing of one kind or another from an early age, whether it is "America the Beautiful" at school or religious music at a church or synagogue. When we attend sports events as a child, we reveal our voices during the national anthem. In all of the above situations, I discovered at an early age that if I sang with my full voice, I would attract a great deal of attention. I quickly learned to either pretend to sing or to sing out with confidence, depending on how I felt that day. To this day, I often do not sing with my full voice during the national anthem or another public song when I am in close proximity to other audience members, unless I am prepared for the attention.

For many years I was inclined to avoid attracting attention to my voice, a sign that perhaps I was not meant to be a full-time performer. Most singers seek out the spotlight. For me, singing began as a deeply personal activity, one in which I felt more vulnerable than at any other time. As a child, I had to be begged to sing in front of anyone. My singing thereafter has been shaped to a large extent by that vulnerability, in both positive and negative ways. The positive effect of my vocal vulnerability has been a certain unique color in my voice that is somehow more open than I am as a person in everyday life.

Jordan says that the real challenge of making honest music is "to recall that experience when you were vulnerable and travel to that place deep within you whenever you make music."[4] What is interesting for me personally is that I feel vulnerable both on and off stage, and this is apparently audible in my voice. It is very difficult for me, however, to be vulnerable in front of an audience. This paradox keeps me excited about performing because I keep striving to allow myself to be as vulnerable as my voice is, and I strive for this in my real life as well.

When we sing, we cannot completely hide our true selves unless we choose to express nothing but technique. Even then, our distance from the music reveals something about us as people. Our bodies and souls comprise our instruments and our hearts have an intangible way of shining forth in our tone quality. Most of the truly warm, generous singers I know sing as they are, while those who are trapped in tight, self-serving patterns sing with a cold, steely tone. Our very physical, human connection to our instruments is the envy of most other instrumentalists, for whom "singing" is the gold standard.

The natural paradox here is that while we cannot conceal our true selves when we sing, we often find it extremely difficult to invest ourselves emotionally in the music. It is much easier to focus infinitely on our technical imperfections than it is to explore our emotions about the music. I know several singers who are hysterically funny and engaging until they begin singing, and then they close down their personalities. Somewhere along the line they learned that it was safer to be like everyone else than it was to capitalize on their individuality. We need this individuality of tone and interpretation, however, to separate ourselves from the rest of the pack. We also need it to feel naturally confident. We don't have to be afraid when we remember that no one else has our voice, our life experiences, and our particular approach to this music. We can be most successfully competitive when we rest in our uniqueness rather than comparing ourselves to others. Our ease with ourselves also makes it easier for us to be gracious toward other singers, a quality that incidentally helps us continue to get hired.

Approaching from the Other Side

One summer I stayed with an extraordinary family while I performed at the Ash Lawn-Highland Festival in Charlottesville, Virginia. Gabriel Laufer is an engineering professor at the University of Virginia, and his wife, Liora, is a handwriting expert. Liora told me that they selected my housing form from the pile because my handwriting told them that I was neat, intelligent, and organized. She also told me they were surprised that I was a performer because my handwriting revealed a more introverted, detail-oriented person.

Liora Laufer has developed a theory about the personality characteristics that handwriting demonstrates. She believes that it may be possible to address some of these character issues by going backward and changing the handwriting patterns first. Her program, called "Callirobics," uses repetitive exercises designed to help her students change particular characteristics. The student follows the example of a word or letter, writing numerous repetitions of the new pattern. By changing the student's handwriting patterns, Liora is able to help the student alter emotional patterns. The program also uses music to accompany the exercises. She has found this program to be highly successful in helping hyperactive children, shy children, and adults with a variety of emotional issues.

I have found that I am sometimes able to help myself or my students develop areas of confidence using a similar technique. One of my acting teachers told me that "acting is pretending." Being a heart-on-my-sleeve kind of person, I was reluctant to view acting this way. I wanted to approach everything from the method acting perspective, feeling everything I sang. Sometimes I achieved beautiful things, particularly when I was singing of sorrow or innocence. I was much less successful communicating happier, less serious emotions that went against my familiar experiences. Not surprisingly, my students all tend toward one end of this spectrum or the other. Some of them are more comfortable with slow, sad pieces, while others relate more naturally to joyful, ebullient material.

For a production of *Albert Herring*, I sang the role of Miss Wordsworth, a fast-moving, perky character. I began telling myself before each rehearsal that I didn't have to actually be happy to properly present this character; I could simply put her on for a while. I even jogged in place to give myself a faster sense of physical energy before I walked out onstage, much to the amusement of my colleagues. Those rehearsals were a turning point for me in the way I approached my acting, as I became quite successful in adapting

Miss Wordsworth's tempo and mood. Before long, my spirits lightened a bit, and I was even able to enjoy the process.

The same principle works in the area of confidence and changing one's expectations for a performance. Sometimes we don't feel secure about an upcoming performance, yet we are nevertheless contracted to perform. If we can convince ourselves to think about the music and the words rather than keeping a running tally in our minds, we can more readily draw the audience into our thoughts. Performances don't have to feel like jury examinations. The audience is not the enemy, despite the undeniable fact that some of its members will surely be critical. If we are not prepared to live in the moment and lose ourselves in love with the music, we will be unable to let the audience into our stories.

Recently I sang the soprano role in *Carmina Burana* by Orff at the relatively new Bass Performance Hall in Fort Worth. I was quite nervous about the role, as it is both extremely high and utterly exposed, and it had been several years since I last sang it. My pianist friend Greg Ritchey gave me the perfect advice. Either I could worry about every note and count the seconds until it was all over, or I could enjoy the performance, knowing that it's not every day that I get to sing a piece I love in such a beautiful hall. The choice was mine. As I stood backstage, I struggled with my dual emotions. I tried to breathe calmly and to remember how excited I was to do this piece again in this particular hall, my favorite in the Dallas-Fort Worth area. I had a fantastic time that weekend, and I did some of the freest, most adventurous singing I'd ever done. Nothing had changed except my mindset about the performance.

Religion and Humility

As a university professor in Texas, I have had many students who struggle with confidence because it seems to conflict with their religious beliefs. Pride is a heinous sin for these students, and they often find it difficult to differentiate between pride and confidence. I assure them that using the gift God gave to them honors Him. Hiding their voices implies that they created them, rather than having received them as a blessing from God. During a master class at Curtis with the great Todd Duncan (the originator of the role of Porgy in Gershwin's *Porgy and Bess*), I heard him say to one of the exceptional students, after pausing for a long moment:

> With a voice like that, it's important not to do anything that's ordinary, not to do anything that's commonplace, because it shows up in a minute, with a voice like that. 'Cause it's a gift, and it can be taken away.

Mr. Duncan's words have always stayed with me. Despite my efforts to convey his meaning, some of my students are also tempted to use an aversion to pride to avoid dealing with other reasons for low self-esteem.

I understand their struggle. During my years in Philadelphia I had several friends who thought it was wrong for me to have a job as a church soloist, to take money for my gift. At the time, I was singing at an Episcopal Church and attending a different church in the evening. I tried to explain that God gave me this voice, and I knew that my voice helped others to be uplifted during the service. I was also a student who needed the money, and, after all, no one expects clergy to work without pay. These days I attend a small Episcopal Church, where I sit out in the congregation. Among them, I can help others feel secure enough to sing out, and I can worship without worrying about the job.

I also believe it is important to minister to others in this world by example. The world of classical music, like many other competitive professions, can be vicious and unforgiving. My students at the University of North Texas have already begun to deal with examples of ungraciousness. I remind them that it is important to be able to look at yourself in the mirror at the end of the day, as my father often said. The others expect you to be drawn into behaving in an equally nasty way, in part because that helps them to justify their own behavior. I suggest that you offer another way to treat other people. Not only is it a way to minister by example, it will also help you to leave these encounters with your heart and self-respect intact.

The operatic world is a secular one, but you can exercise your spirituality through the way you choose to interact with others.

Singers of all faiths go through times in their lives when ego issues, as well as artistic issues, become problematic. The difficulty can be something as straightforward as not wanting to miss Sunday morning services (or Friday evening services) for an opera rehearsal or as complex as not wanting to sing about a rape. One of the sopranos at Curtis singing the role of the Female Chorus in Britten's *The Rape of Lucretia* had a very difficult time with the material. I sang the role of the maid, Lucia, and I was never able to watch the rape scene, primarily because my boyfriend at the time was singing the role of the rapist (Tarquinius). Most operatic material is not terrifically extreme, however, and every singer works out these spiritual and moral issues as they arise during his or her career.

Competitive Jealousy

In her recent book, *Emotional Alchemy*, Tara Bennett-Goleman discusses various emotional patterns, including competitive jealousy and its effects on professional pursuits:

> Jealousy and envy revolve around comparing oneself to others and judging them. At an extreme, this becomes resentment of the accomplishments of others and a paranoid fear that others will outdo one. This judgmental attitude breeds condescension and a flurry of activity around setting things right—that is, in accord with one's own view of how things should be—and so imposing one's own order.[5]

Like any strong emotion, however, envy can work either negatively or positively in the singer. Bennett-Goleman continues, "When transformed, this busy energy becomes competence, allowing activities to flourish effectively. Action becomes well aimed, opportunities are seized, and the possibilities inherent in a moment become actualized."[6] Envy can cripple one singer while it drives another to work harder. Competitive jealousy should not be the primary motivation for one's career as an artist, although it plays an important role. Most singers will admit to having become more eager to sing when they consider the preceding singer to be less skilled than they are. The opposite situation is rarely true. When another singer delivers a "perfect" performance or exhibits a tone we wish we could emulate, we seldom feel energized to jump into the arena. If someone else suggests that another singer is better, and we don't share that opinion, we generally do sing with heightened excitement and motivation. Soprano Patricia Racette has said that her first classical teacher used flattery of other sopranos as a tool for fueling Racette's own performances.

The most effective teacher uses studio classes and other group situations to build confidence and to create a supportive environment. Singers, like regular people, tend to conform to the norms and values of their social group, i.e., other singers. It is important not to create a star system, but to acknowledge the different levels of advancement within the studio. Creating social events for the group helps to foster the idea that these values are held by all. Every person in the studio must know that he or she is equally important to the teacher and worthy as a human being.

Being open about all vocal issues, including your own, is one way to create an atmosphere of trust. I learned this lesson while student teaching under James Jordan, then at Lewisburg High School. On this particular day, I listened to one of his students sing a piece completely out of tune from beginning to end. He asked me what I thought. I hesitated for a long moment and then stammered out something incoherent about [u] vowels and minor thirds within a smaller range. Dr. Jordan and the student shared a secret smile, and then he told her to move to the other side of the piano. This time she sang perfectly on pitch. Again, he asked me for an opinion, but I was speechless. Then he explained that she was deaf in one ear.

There were many lessons in that story, not the least of which being that I should look for creative solutions and treat every student as an individual. But mostly what I took away was that we could be completely frank about the student's vocal difficulties and deal with them as a group in a way that freed her from any embarrassment or shame. This lesson influenced every day of my teaching life from that day forward. My students have learned that their vocal issues will all be openly discussed, as will mine, and their vocal strengths will also be fair game.

I find that assigning the same piece to two people at different levels can be another effective way to teach authentic confidence. Recently, I presented some of this material at a conference for teachers, and one of the teachers suggested that this might simply engender more competition between singers. In practice, it depends on how the teacher manages the situation. I always choose two students with very different instruments, usually at widely varying points in their studies. They learn that perfect technique is not the only thing that makes the piece effective. By investing themselves in the piece, they can make it their own, and every individual can have a valid interpretation. In this way all of the students in the class learn not to fear comparison with others.

Sometimes magic happens in studio class, and a student goes further emotionally than she ever has before. On one such day, Marissa got up to sing Schumann's "Heiss mich nicht reden," from *Mignon Lieder*. Marissa's father, living on the other side of the country, had become ill, her mother had recently gone into remission from her own illness, and the date for her masters recital was rapidly approaching. She began to sing but was soon overcome by tears. I asked her to stay up there, knowing that if she sat down it would be infinitely harder for her ever to perform this piece again. If she cried during the song, I said, that would be fine. She should just let it happen, listen to Natasha play, and sing whenever she could. I didn't care if she sang a single note.

Marissa began the piece again, and she cried almost continuously, but she never completely stopped singing. It was one of the most gripping performances I have ever seen. She connected with the inner depths of her voice in ways I had not thought possible. The class was stunned. All of the students wanted to get up and sing their most emotional pieces after that. Everyone cried, and it was truly a day to remember. One of my smartest but most emotionally controlled undergraduates, Dianna, sang her own Schumann in what was a complete transformation. Both of their recitals a month later were utter surprises to me in the levels of artistry and communication these singers were able to achieve. I can't wait to see where they will go next.

I would not have had the confidence to keep Marissa onstage through her tears were it not for a similar experience I'd had as a graduate student at Curtis. We were rehearsing the famous trio from *Der Rosenkavalier* by Richard Strauss, in which I was singing the role of Sophie. The music was so beautiful, and I was having an emotional day anyway. At the end of the trio I started weeping and was unable to stop. Danielle Orlando, our coach, continued to play as we went on into the duet. The mezzo-soprano singing Octavian, Charlotte Hellekant, simply walked over to me and put her arm around me, singing the duet alone while I cried. The rehearsal ended, and no one said anything to me about my outburst.

Several months later at another program, Danielle mentioned that day to me. I turned eighteen shades of red and began to apologize. Danielle interrupted and said, "No, that was the day I knew you were an artist. I was starting to wonder whether or not there was anything in you." Up to that point I had been very shy and emotionally blank when I sang. Apparently it had been difficult to see my sensitivity and passion for music. Now I am not disconcerted if a student is moved deeply enough to weep. I am more worried if I never see any emotional display at all.

Making the Music Bigger Than We Are

For me, the best way to keep perspective on my ego is to remember that the music is the reason I am on the stage. Being competitive with others helps us to seek our personal best in order to meet higher standards. Art is empty, however, if it is not created out of love and selflessness. The music is bigger than we are, I tell my students, and we are the custodians of this beautiful, classical art form. If we perform because we love the applause and the attention, we will cheat ourselves of the joy given to us by genuine love for the music. I first began to feel my responsibility to the art form one night onstage as Susanna in the Act IV Finale of Mozart's *Le nozze di Figaro.* As we sang the glorious "Ah, tutti contenti," I began to think about the fact that singers had sung these roles for hundreds of years before me and would continue to sing them long after I was gone. I suddenly knew that I was part of a tradition much larger than I was. I had similar feelings of privilege while singing Lucia's famous "Mad Scene." This awareness has continued to have great meaning for me both spiritually and musically.

It is all too easy to lose sight of what is important in the microcosms of our individual schools, no matter how large or small they may be. I think this is one thing the conservatories do very well: they conserve (keep, or save) the art form. Curtis was a highly competitive place in terms of gaining acceptance, but within its walls the focus was entirely on music: creating the truest, clearest, most personal, most stylistic music. It was never about producing sounds for the sake of the singer's ego alone, or the pianist's, or the violinist's, or anyone else's. One became a star at Curtis by training to be a sophisticated, nuanced musician and by using superior technique to achieve world-class musical results.

As I try to teach my students to put the music ahead of their own ambitions and to let the rest follow, I am reminded of Viktor Frankl's words. The renowned Austrian psychologist wrote in *Man's Search for Meaning,* his 1959 book about his imprisonment during the Holocaust:

> Don't aim at success—the more you aim at it and make it a target, the more you are going to miss it. For success, like happiness, cannot be pursued; it must ensue....as the unintended side effect of one's personal dedication to a course greater than oneself.[7]

When we are able to put the music first, we have an easier time remembering why we initially chose to be musicians, and we find happiness in a much more honest way.

Notes

1. James Jordan, *The Musician's Soul* (Chicago: GIA Publications, Inc., 1998).
2. Ibid., 111–116.
3. Ibid., 109.
4. Ibid., 33.
5. Tara Bennett-Goleman, *Emotional Alchemy* (New York: Harmony Books, 2001), 313.
6. Ibid.
7. Victor Emil Frankl, *Man's Search for Meaning*, Revised and Updated (New York: Washington Square Press, 1997).

Further Exploration

1. When did you first receive attention from others because of your voice?

   _____

   _____

   What feelings did you have about it then? Now?

   _____

   _____

2. Using one sentence or less, describe the best thing about your voice.

   _____

   Look at your answer. Did you define your strength in comparison to others?

   _____

   What is your best quality as a person? _____
   Do people who hear you sing come away knowing this about you?

   _____

3. Choose two pieces from your repertoire, one that reflects your typical mood and one that is less familiar to your personality.

   1)_____
   2)_____

   What aspects of your emotional life will you use to represent the text in the first piece? In the less familiar piece, what emotion will you have to "pretend?" For the second piece, can you think of a person in your life who would act that way?

   1)_____
   2)_____

4. Write down words you associate with the word "pride."

_____

_____

How do these words relate to your feelings about your voice?

_____

_____

5. Do you ever sing in religious settings? _____
How (if at all) are these experiences different emotionally than other kinds of performances?

_____

_____

_____

6. Name five singers whom you envy. They can be famous singers, but at least one should be someone you know personally and hear on a regular basis.

(1)_____

(2) _____

(3) _____

(4) _____

(5) _____

What types of things do you envy about them? Does your envy inspire you to work harder, or does it make you want to give up?

_____

_____

_____

_____

7. When I am one of a group of singers performing on a program, I am most motivated to get up and sing when (choose one):

_____the singer before me is not as good as I am.

_____the singer before me is better than I am.

8. Have you ever been moved to tears while singing? Describe the experience. Did it affect your ability to be vulnerable onstage in later performances?

_____

_____

_____

_____

_____

9. What is your dream role or piece? _____

Name at least three famous interpreters of the role or work. (Do some homework if necessary!)

_____

_____

_____

What do you hope to bring to the role or piece if you are fortunate enough to have the opportunity to sing it?

_____

_____

_____

_____

_____

Chapter Three: Artistic Ownership—Comfort Levels

Patrick Gnage, a former student of renowned tenor Seth Mc-Coy's, shared one of his teacher's insights with me: "Sing to express, not to impress." Is what we choose to express based in the music or in ourselves? The answer to this question doesn't come easily, and in the silence another question appears. Do we believe the music is more important than we are? We may feel that we "interpret" the composer's intentions through our life experiences, but we may not see their importance as anything other than a reflective surface. As I struggle to clarify the difference for myself and for my students, I increasingly wonder what we have to give up to put music first and why we don't all want to do so naturally. I suspect that artistic ownership is defined by the answers to these questions.

As we interpret a piece of music, we translate the composer's intentions into terms that have meaning for us. Interpretation is influenced by many factors, all of which can be considered to fall within the interpreter's "world view." Our life experiences contribute most obviously to our world view, which can be further divided into subcategories such as moral and spiritual beliefs, interaction with other art forms, and present-day emotional lives. All of these factors (and countless others) impact every artistic decision we make, both consciously and subconsciously.

When considering the idea of comfort levels with regard to art istic ownership, many questions come to mind. Do we see what we do as the artistic expression of our beliefs about the world or as a disconnected escape from them? Do our musical experiences change us as people? Do we allow them to change us? I know that I have been profoundly changed by certain singing experiences and completely untouched by others. Sometimes I feel my singing as an expression of my deepest beliefs, freely offered in a way that engages my whole self more fully than mere words ever could. At other times my voice and I are two separate entities, and in those moments I am on musicians' gig autopilot.

I have found that some of my purest, most generous singing happens in situations in which I don't know any of the audience members. I have been singing solo recitals at the Hudební Festival Vysocina, a regional festival in the Czech Republic, for the past three summers. The venues vary greatly from town to town, as do the audiences. It is liberating for me to know that there will be no critique—no review (at least not one that I will be able to read), no colleagues, no students looking to my example. It is simply about the music. During those performances I know that music is the only language I have with which to communicate, and I am able to give more from my heart and soul. I return from these trips refreshed and ready to immerse myself in the academic world again.

It does seem clear that certain types of people choose to become performing artists. One brand of singer enters the profession hoping for personal attention, performing a task onstage to receive a reward (applause, etc.). These singers are generally not interested in creating artistic colors for their own sake. They don't understand why other singers waste valuable time on this unless it will make them stand out of the crowd even more brilliantly. Unfortunately, these singers have become the stereotypes, the singers who sing for their own personal glory rather than for genuine love of the music.

My experience as a teacher suggests that the singers who possess the richest, most beautiful singing voices are themselves the most soulful, most emotionally complex people. These singers, when they are able to sing who they truly are, convey worlds of spiritual depth within the colors of their voices. Some of them are more comfortable with this kind of exposure before an audience than others, and are therefore more able to share and develop their gifts. The issue of comfort levels can be a means of natural selection for artists.

Temperament and Repertoire

The attention we spend learning our craft (language, articulation, style, and so forth) serves to help us define the artistic situations in which we are most comfortable. Ultimately the question always returns to our reasons for singing in the first place. Do we work on all of these elements of singing to get attention in as highly visible a venue as possible? Or do we refine ourselves because we are fascinated by music, we want to spend hours and hours finding just the right colors even if no hears us, and we also know that we will get attention if we play our cards right?

It may be a question of temperament. I have heard the terms *Stimmdiva* and *Kunstdiva* mentioned by several opera singers. In preparing for the role of Marguerite in Gounod's *Faust*, the *Stimmdiva* (voice-*diva*) orders her outfits and learns her cadenzas. The *Kunstdiva* (art-*diva*) reads the original Goethe. This is an oversimplification, to be sure, but most singers fall more closely into one category or the other. Today's operatic singer needs to do all of these things to be successful.

The singer's temperament, the old nature vs. nurture debate aside, is fairly well established by the time he or she begins formal study. The longer I teach, the more convinced I am that people sing as they are, that they sing what is in their hearts. One type of singer focuses exclusively on the external elements of singing, such as the attire, the technical perfection, or the attitude. But another category of artists searches beyond this level for the internal truths about music, always striving for honest emotion (both theirs and the composer's) and meaningful tone color. It is very difficult to convince a singer from one camp that the other is important, particularly for those who wish to avoid internal examination. The true artist's temperament does not dwell within every musician, unfortunately, and some musicians know only that they "don't have it," whatever "it" actually is.

The singers who search for the truest sound dig ever deeper into their own hearts and minds until they say what it is they have come to the stage to say. They are never satisfied with mere competency, and they repeat phrases over and over searching for emotional truth. Their voices never sound "hollow," a word one of my students used to describe a singer who did not sound present in her own voice. Are their voices colorful because they work so hard to infuse the music with emotional content? Or are their voices colorful because they are fascinating, special people at their very core, and their personal light shines through in their singing? In my opinion, the answer lies in some combination of these two ideas. Genuine artists are complex, spiritual, generous people who work diligently to bring themselves into every aspect of their art. No artist can hide behind superficial trappings and ever approach true satisfaction of interpretation. For this reason, not everyone is comfortable being an artist, and many people are content merely to be singers.

Repertoire is often the most obvious way to accommodate our comfort levels. As a young singer I was very comfortable with my upper range and flexibility and less sure of my middle voice and dramatic ability. I chose arias that allowed me to float numerous high notes without having to be too spunky or interesting as an actress. My voice and I seemed to merge into the perfect bland young ingénue. I loved "Caro nome," for example, while I was scared to death of "Je suis Titania," even though it was easier for me vocally, because I lacked the confidence to sell the latter aria properly. It wasn't until I began my doctoral study that I discovered how much more interesting it was to choose music for the text.

Now that I am a university professor, of course, I have much more control over what I sing and how I sing it, which is definitely a comfort level choice for me. In my former life as an opera singer, I wasn't happy saying "Yes, maestro" all of the time; I wanted to make some of the musical decisions. Although I enjoy the conductors I work with now immensely, I enjoy my recital work as well. My current musical life is a satisfactory balance of orchestral work, both modern and Baroque, and recitals in various formats. All artists have to find the right balance of projects for themselves, which can be (and hopefully will be) a lifelong task.

Everything that affects our interpretation of a piece affects our artistic ownership of it, including our moral and spiritual beliefs. Recently, one of my sopranos brought in Mahler's setting of "Liebst du um Schönheit" from *Rückert-Lieder*:

Liebst du um Schönheit, o nicht mich liebe!	If you love for beauty, O love not me!
Liebe die Sonne, sie trägt ein goldnes Haar!	Love the sun, she has golden hair!
Liebst du um Jugend, o nicht mich liebe!	If you love for youth, O love not me!
Liebe den Frühling, der jung ist jedes Jahr!	Love the spring who is young each year!
Liebst du um Schätze, o nicht mich liebe!	If you love for riches, o love not me!
Liebe die Meerfrau, sie hat viel Perlen klar!	Love the mermaid who has many pearls!
Liebst du um Liebe, o ja – mich liebe!	If you love for love, oh yes, love me!
Liebe mich immer, dich lieb ich immerdar!	Love me ever, I'll love you always!

My student focused on the idea that it was morally wrong to love all of these external things more than love itself, which may perhaps be the poet's point. With this view in mind, however, she colored the words *Schönheit, Sonne, Jugend*, etc., with a scornful tone that did not consider the depth of Mahler's music. We discussed various degrees of interpretation, including the idea that judgment may not be the primary intent of the poem. She commented on her conservative, religious west Texas upbringing and the ways it affects her thinking, consciously and subconsciously.

Many of the most profound works in the vocal repertoire are unsuitable for students because of their interpretative difficulty. I often find myself telling a student that her piece will feel entirely different ten years from now, and then her feelings will change about it again in another ten years. Sometimes I want to tell them that they won't truly understand this poem until something really bad happens to them. Every singer and teacher should consider whether their life experiences will give them enough of what they need to relate to particular poems and pieces.

A Word on Performance Anxiety

Performance anxiety is a growing problem for today's professional musicians. I believe that many performance anxiety issues stem from basic ego problems, such as lack of self-esteem, confusing the voice with the self, and the absence of a clear desire to perform. At the University of North Texas, we recently incorporated a related field in music and medicine as an option at the doctoral level to encourage research on some of these issues. The best antidotes I know to singers' performance fears, however, are thorough preparation and commitment to the text, which leave nothing else for the singer to think about while singing.

Some of my students are initially more nervous during their lessons than they are during performances. When they refuse to give more of themselves to the music, they tell me, "I'll do it in the performance." Many of them will be more animated and free in the performance because they know they will not be interrupted and critiqued along the way. This method of learning to perform is too haphazard to be truly effective. A true artist stops caring about what people think long before the performance. The focus has to be on the process and on doing everything possible to interpret the piece effectively.

All singers must know themselves with unsparing clarity in order to fight performance anxiety successfully. I am not yet convinced that it is useful for a performer to determine that he suffers from a condition called "performance anxiety," for this determination accepts the inevitability of incapacitating fear in every performance situation, regardless of the circumstances. It also removes responsibility from the singer. It becomes easier to blame the condition than to take action to address the emotional factors that created the fear. Some singers never experience these fears—they seem born to walk out onto the stage. These fortunate individuals aside, most of us encounter feelings of self-doubt at some point, and we don't have to allow these doubts to snowball into a full-blown condition.

Beta-blockers have become a common solution to the problem, but while they are helpful to many performers, they alleviate the symptoms without ever touching on the root causes of the anxiety. While these drugs calm the nerves, they also deaden the musician's sense of tempo and musical passion. Most of the singers I know who use these drugs have ambivalent feelings about the necessary sacrifices.

I have never been a natural performer. I have always been a quiet, shy, bookish person who happened to be blessed with a beautiful singing voice. Fortunately for me, I have almost always trusted my voice, even if I lacked confidence about virtually everything else. I hated to get up in front of people to speak, but as soon as I began to sing, my nerves evaporated. Like many successful young singers, I instinctively knew certain things about singing, and I was lucky enough to have early teachers who didn't try to manipulate my natural sound. When I performed in my first opera at nineteen, I was overjoyed because I was able to sing everything (as opposed to the musicals I had been doing, in which I had spoken lines). I struggled for years with my hatred of performing, pursuing it only because I loved the musical process and because people kept telling me I had the talent to do it.

Today I am much more at ease with my performing self. I have learned that I am not a performer by nature but that I can improve both my skill and my enjoyment onstage. I have also learned that my talent doesn't obligate me to devote myself to a career that isn't right for me personally. Since I internalized these truths, I have become much less ambivalent about performing. As soon as I entered the doctoral program at Florida State University and allowed myself to engage in activities outside of performance, I began to perform more joyfully. Through two outstanding teachers there, my voice teacher Yvonne Ciannella and stage director Michael McConnell, I found that communication skills could be learned after all, and I began to see a world of new possibilities in music. Soon I was so immersed in making artistic choices through my texts that I had little time onstage for self-flagellation.

Technique

"Interpretation can sometimes get in the way of good technique," I once read on a student's sheet of comments from a voice teacher. It is undoubtedly true that excessive emotion can disturb proper vocal production. This statement reads, however, as though technique is the goal. We must remember that good technique is desirable because it allows us a wider spectrum of artistic choices. Vocal production for its own sake is empty and generic unless it has a musical purpose.

It is very easy to hide behind the search for technical perfection, with the intent to begin the artistic process on the day when technical perfection is finally achieved. Unfortunately, technical perfection is an unattainable goal, and if a singer approaches a performance hoping to achieve it, he guarantees disappointment and failure. For all too many singers, this means that the artistic process never begins in any meaningful way because there is always more work to do on one's breath support or *passaggio* or whatever problem will become this week's reason to postpone becoming an artist. Working with these problems will either allow us to hide or free us to communicate.

Technique should not be viewed as separate from artistry; rather, the two have a symbiotic relationship. Yvonne Ciannella always told me, "Sing your technique musically, and sing your music technically." It took me a relatively long time to decipher what that truly meant. At first she asked me to "perform" my exercises, assigning emotions or colors to each cadenza. I was terribly shy about doing this in her presence—and weren't we just warming up anyway? Finally she convinced me to try keeping my eyes alive while I sang, a manageable task for even the most reticent student. Doing this changed my sound radically, to my surprise. She referred to this as the "X factor," adding the personal artistry without which singing remains scientific and never reaches the realm of true art. According to James Jordan, fine teachers and conductors are aware when the "X factor" is not present:

> Many times there is something missing in the sound: that something
> which provides a brilliance of color and accuracy of pitch...a human-
> ness to the sound...born because of the conductor's selflessness and
> understanding of human love through music.[1]

In the practice room, I experimented with keeping my eyes animated, eventually graduating to fuller facial expressions of joy. Whenever I reached a technical impasse with an exercise, I tried abandoning the technique and simply singing a joyous cadenza. At least nine times out of ten, this change in attitude freed up my instrument enough to produce the sound I wanted. I gathered up the courage to begin doing this during my lessons, and Miss Ciannella began to introduce me to the many available colors of my voice using different emotional contexts.

This discovery had lasting effects on my approach to repertoire. For years, coaches and directors had been telling me that I made beautiful sounds with admirable technical control but my singing lacked emotional content. I became quite frustrated; as an intelligent, feeling person, I certainly understood what I was singing, and I thought I was doing everything I could to express that. I didn't have the tools for doing more until I started thinking about the individual words and how I might use their colors to keep my technique flexible. Soon I began dealing with problems from both sides. If my ideas about physical technique weren't effective, I tried to forget about them and merely color the words instead. Reversing this process when the emotions made me sloppy ensured that I would stay as balanced as I was expressive.

Simply thinking about an emotion is hardly a substitute for a solid technical base. There comes a point in every singer's life, however, when it is appropriate to stop thinking about the mechanics and start making art. If the singer never reaches this point, he or she has no way to truly stand out from thousands of other young singers. We cannot access our most individual, most honest sound until we release ourselves to the task of communicating the music, putting aside our obsession with the ways others view us. This takes practice, however, and we must be disciplined about it.

In his book *Complications: A Surgeon's Notes on an Imperfect Science*, surgeon Atul Gawande discusses studies done on elite performers in a variety of fields, finding that the amount of practice is the biggest difference between them and less distinguished performers.[2] Gawande goes on to cite the work of K. Anders Ericsson, a cognitive psychologist and performance expert:

> The most important way in which innate factors play a role may be in one's willingness to engage in sustained training...Top performers dislike practicing just as much as others do...But more than others, they have the will to keep at it anyway.[3]

Tolerance for practice and self-discipline are connected with perfectionism, a trait with positive and negative ramifications for its bearer. Perfectionist musicians will spend many hours practicing their instrument, but they may not practice with intelligence and efficiency. Singers in this group continue to practice long after the voice is spent, and they practice on days when the instrument is compromised by poor health or fatigue. For singers, the discipline has to rest in study more than in actual time on the voice because we are limited by our instruments' physical endurance. Many singers spend significantly more time worrying about the function of their voices on any given day than they do practicing or studying. When we perform, we may worry (as all musicians do) that we will destroy the performance at any moment with something less than perfect. We should accept from the outset that nothing we do will be perfect and free ourselves to make music instead. I am often relieved when I make an error in performance because I am then officially released from the self-imposed pressure to give a perfect rendition of the piece.

Stylistic Truth

Our sense of artistic ownership reveals itself clearly in our stylistic truthfulness and our comfort with various styles. Many singers fear that they will damage their instruments by singing different styles, including jazz, musical theater, popular music, and even the classical works of earlier composers, such as Handel or Mozart. This concern only has merit if they sing Mozart or Gershwin as though their works were the same as Puccini's. Mozart's music (and Gershwin's music, for that matter) was not designed to accommodate frequent use of *portamento* or vibrato around the pitch instead of through its center. The singer who ignores these realities will not sound convincing and will ultimately struggle with the music's contours. On the other hand, one can readily see why a cleaner, drier approach to the sound would not be effective in Puccini's music.

These differences manifest themselves in the efficient use of technique, even as there must be consistency in the basic function of the instrument across all repertoire. I regularly sing both early and modern classical repertoire, and while I am periodically accused of singing with completely different techniques for different pieces, I have also been asked to give classes on how to handle both successfully. (In both cases, I am gratified that my efforts have been noticed.) The ping-pong paddle and the tennis racket share basic structural elements, such as the handle and the rounded surface with which to hit the ball across the net. That said, one would never think of using these rackets interchangeably for either game. In singing we cannot let go of the fundamental processes of breath and resonance, regardless of what we are attempting to sing. Yet it makes little sense to approach all repertoire as though it were Italian opera.

For some voice professionals, choosing repertoire means first determining whether you have a ping-pong paddle or a tennis racket, or a baseball bat, or something else. Many decisions have already been made for us by Nature, and we must know how our voices best fit the material. Within these categories, however, we still have many different options. Singing is not a sport. It is an artistic endeavor; therefore, we cannot limit ourselves to a single approach. Even golfers, whose goal is arguably more objective, use a variety of different clubs.

Understanding how to sing stylistically begins with knowledge of what differentiates the styles. If we don't know which elements are specific to the style, we cannot begin to capture its essence. For example, many singers think that early music is characterized simply by straight tone, and they don't wish to "shave" their voices to produce that. If they are required to sing with a straighter tone, they stop the air and clamp down on their throats, a process that surely endangers their vocal survival. What truly separates earlier styles from late nineteenth-century styles, though, is clarity of pitch. Most early music conductors care a great deal more about intonation than anything else. Some of the figures in this music require less vibrato to properly differentiate the pitches. Surely it is not damaging to the instrument to sing in tune. Beyond that, one has to be aware that faster air and attention to pitch can help produce a straighter tone at times without clamping down in any way. Articulation is another word for this, particularly with regard to weight. One has to understand which notes are important rather than working to keep every pitch equally open and loud, an unmusical approach to material in any style.

The other, perhaps more important, consideration is the use of language. Instrumentalists often say they wish they had text with which to communicate. Yet many singers view the words as obstacles to their own glorious tones. They are afraid to truly pronounce the words, preferring barely to touch on the consonants and keep all vowels in the same [ah] position. We do sing on vowels, and we should attempt to create a steady resonance. However, by avoiding the consonants altogether we don't take advantage of the many voiced consonants in our texts. Proper placement of these consonants and the vowels (particularly the higher, more closed vowels) adds to the vertical space in the tone. The voiced consonants also help us form legato lines.

True legato is formed by matching resonance. If you form one space and force all of the vowels to conform to that space, the resonance bounces all around in the head. The color of the vowel may stay the same, but this will only seem to be true because it is a "uni-vowel" (one vowel for all). The diction is poor, and true resonance is sacrificed. For me, that is "band-aid legato." Real legato happens when you adjust the space from vowel to vowel in order to match the resonance. When the resonance is consistent, the singer has a much better chance of being heard over the orchestra. This balanced resonance is equally attainable in every major singing language.

"The language *is* the style," as Yvonne Ciannella often said. When the language of the piece is properly produced without being forced into a general "Italianate" space, the piece assumes much of its natural flavor immediately. Nowhere is this more true than in the detailed form of art song, yet this principle holds true to a lesser degree in other genres, including opera. It is equally difficult to imagine either Figaro's "Largo al factotum" from *Il barbiere di Siviglia* by Rossini or the great Lied "Erlkönig" by Schubert sung in any other language. We smile at the thought, but we must ask ourselves why the language itself is so critical to the piece's texture.

These considerations have technical ramifications for the singer. The singer must learn how to produce each one of the major singing languages without compromising his other central technique. I maintain that it is actually easier, not more difficult, when one commits completely to the special characteristics of each language. These pieces were written to be sung in these languages, and singing them all using the same round production makes them tougher to negotiate, just as using a tennis racket to play ping pong would severely handicap the player. Learning each language's details requires greater preparation at the outset, but this work can save the singer hours of time in lining up their voice later on in the process.

For me, the key to organizing the particulars of each language into something manageable has been the idea that each language tastes different in my mouth. That is to say, the shapes I'm making have their own images and colors specific to that language. Within the general taste, I can fine-tune infinitely without losing the broader sense of the language's flow. I use several shapes as starting points for my students; these are the areas of resonance that they must work hard to keep open at all times in order to maintain the flavor of each language. For French, I use an egg sitting upright in the front of my mouth. For German, I picture a small balloon sitting up on a shelf in the back of my head, as in the first syllable of the word *alles*. Italian requires an awareness of roundness throughout the space, as though one's head were a beach ball.

The next question my students inevitably ask is what shape might describe the primary resonance for English. English is difficult because it incorporates elements of all three languages, mostly French and German, and mixes them together to make shapes of its own. (The shapes for all of these languages vary greatly from north to south, region to region, ranging up to variances as great as British vs. American English.) The singer who ignores the special resonance for French and German, singing everything as though it were in Italian, is rarely intelligible. Furthermore, the sound is not as beautiful as it could be because it settles for one homogenized color rather than attempting to explore the many possible colors of the given language.

As a student at the European Center for Opera and Vocal Arts in Belgium one summer, I observed a master class with Italian baritone Elio Battaglia. A young baritone from Prague presented "Non più andrai," from Act I of Mozart's *Le nozze di Figaro* in Italian. His presentation was completely devoid of character or dramatic interest, leading Mr. Battaglia to ask him if he had ever sung the role. "Oh yes, many times with the Prague National Opera," the young singer replied. "But we sing in Czech there." Mr. Battaglia asked him to show us. This time the singer was much more animated, and his Figaro sprang to life immediately. Of course, it was incredibly odd from an aural perspective, but the singer's enthusiasm and commitment made his version viable. There are many lessons in this story, but my point here is that this singer had not been properly trained to sing and communicate in other languages, with nearly disastrous results.

At the professional level, the question of style becomes more critical. The ability to separate and define different musical styles is based in a highly detailed knowledge of music. Even in the field of opera, the days of "park and bark" are coming to an end in all but the largest international houses. The simple economics of the business continue to make ever more minute differences between singers count in hiring decisions. The young singer who wants to make a living in music must become fluent in as many musical languages as possible. The more compelling reason to sing stylistically, however, is that it is infinitely more satisfying and interesting for the singer, as well as the audience. Blaring out a uniform sound may have its momentary rewards, but exploring one's own ideas in a variety of styles and languages results in far more lasting artistic satisfaction.

Notes

1. James Jordan, *The Musician's Soul* (Chicago: GIA Publications, Inc., 1998), 8.
2. Atul Gawande, *Complications* (New York: Metropolitan Books, 2002), 20.
3. Ibid., 20.

Further Exploration

1. List adjectives that describe music you are most comfortable singing.

   _____ _____ _____

   _____ _____ _____

   _____ _____ _____

2. When you begin a new opera aria or role, what is the very first thing you do?

   _____

   _____

   _____

3. What are the two or three main technical issues on which you are currently working?

   (1)_____

   (2) _____

   (3) _____

   How do these technical issues prevent you from doing what you want to do artistically? Be specific about pieces and phrases.

   _____

   _____

   _____

4. Do you spend as much time working on the artistic content of your music (and how you want to communicate that) as you do on the technical aspects? If not, why not?

   _____

   _____

5. Choose an aria from your repertoire that contains cadenzas on the [a] vowel. Experiment with different emotional colors for each one, beginning with keeping your eyes animated. Use the mirror when you are ready.

6. List three composers with whose works you are most comfortable.

_____

_____

_____

List three composers with whose works you are not comfortable.

_____

_____

_____

Compare the two lists. What do they tell you about your singing temperament?

_____

_____

7. What is your favorite language in which to sing?_____
Why?_____

_____

8. *Listening Assignment*: *The Artistry of Elly Ameling* (Philips 473 451–2). This five-CD set is a primer in singing stylistically. Soprano Elly Ameling sails effortlessly through works by Bach, Vivaldi, Handel, Haydn, Mozart, Schumann, Brahms, Wolf, Fauré, Debussy, Hahn, Satie, Gershwin, Porter, and Ellington, capturing the subtle and not-so-subtle differences between them. It is an excellent source for most of her very best recordings.

Chapter Four: Therapy

I once studied with a voice teacher who thought that all singers should go through therapy, not necessarily because of family dysfunction or mental illness, but because we have to know ourselves so well to handle life as singers. We are asked to bare our souls through texts that deal with love, death, and other deeply felt subjects. If we sing opera, we must be physical in all kinds of ways while an audience watches from afar. While some actors enter the profession in order to become someone else, singers seem to have much more trouble separating themselves from their roles. We may have personal issues that keep us from being completely free onstage, issues that have little to do with music or technique. Therapy, like an acting class or a new set of headshots, can become one more part of the singer's preparation for a career.

Many singers find that deep personal issues come to the surface as they navigate the realities of building a career. The countless rejections demoralize us as we begin to attend dozens of auditions, all the more painfully if we equate our voice with ourselves. Once cast in an opera we may be asked to push our emotional boundaries beyond our comfort levels. We may not understand why a particular role or scene is so disturbing to us. If we are having other personal life problems, we will have difficulty singing about related issues, such as lost love. When our own lives mirror the texts too closely, it is hardest of all. Perhaps we had no idea when we started singing that we would have to be quite this naked emotionally. While we want to change our feelings, we may not be able to accomplish this without professional help.

Every singer must come to believe in his or her uniqueness, both vocally and personally, before he or she can go out onstage without baggage. If we cannot believe that we have sensibilities unlike anyone before us, we have little chance of success in the professional world. We may make some gains through imitating others, but that kind of success generally doesn't lead to a long-term solo career. The pyramid narrows as singers keep moving to the top, and many singers are excluded with each new selection process. Each singer must develop something special to survive in competition with hundreds of other equally gifted singers. It often takes quite a long time to find lasting success. As one teacher pointed out, the singers who make it are often the ones who stay with it for years and are patient enough to wait things out.

For some fortunate singers, their early success creates problems. I have one friend who won the Metropolitan Opera National Auditions immediately following his bachelor's degree. He went on to have a highly successful career at the Met and then internationally. A few years ago he told me that he dislikes facing ever rising expectations when he sings, and that it is increasingly difficult for him to enjoy the work. He has begun a second career as a private teacher whenever his schedule permits.

My Own Story

At various times throughout my life, therapy has been an important tool, sometimes directly connected with disappointing life events, but at other times becoming necessary even when I have many reasons to feel blessed. My first experience with "therapy" came at the tender age of seven, growing up on Long Island, New York. As I described in Chapter One, I knew how to read when I entered kindergarten, and this at first made me immensely popular. By the time I reached second grade, however, reading well simply made me a "teacher's pet." My baby sister had just been born, and because I'd recently acquired both glasses and braces, she was by far the more charming girl. On top of all that, my beloved grandparents sold their house in Brooklyn and moved to Florida. I went to several sessions with the school psychologist, who asked me to describe what I saw in inkblots. Whether or not we accomplished anything, I grew to look forward to the sessions, largely because it was pleasant for me to have someone really listen to my problems.

I endured the typically nightmarish years of junior high and high school, suffering from intermittent depression. I'm sure that to others my depression didn't seem much different from the normal adolescent angst because every teenage girl occasionally thinks that she is ugly and fat and that no one will ever love her. To a large extent, it probably was the product of changing hormones. I did have my voice to carry me through, for I was always confident that I had at least one talent that was not typical in any way. I took leading roles often in our high school musicals, so I was part of a socially accepted group. When I see teenage students today, I think that all adults deserve some sort of reward merely for getting through the high school years in one piece.

My second therapeutic experience happened during my years in the master's program at the Curtis Institute of Music. In the fall semester of my final year, I endured several tests of my emotional strength. My on-again, off-again three-year relationship with another singer ended in a very public and prolonged way. At the time, I was singing several outside choral jobs in addition to my responsibilities at Curtis and shouting at my boyfriend whenever I had the time. I walked around all of this pretending I was fine and repressing my emotions quite a bit, even with myself. Eventually I developed blisters on my vocal cords, and my ENT prescribed six weeks of vocal rest to ensure that the blisters would not enlarge into nodules. I had to cancel all of my December auditions for summer programs, and I had to bow out of a gala concert with the Curtis Orchestra in which I was to have sung the Zerbinetta/Composer duet and Zerbinetta's aria from *Ariadne auf Naxos* with guest conductor Max Rudolf. It was for this concert that I had endured everything else that fall, and I saw it as my reward.

I rested through the six weeks, not even singing any Christmas carols, and I sounded better than ever when I resumed after the New Year. I was still uneasy about having done just one audition in February for a summer program, Ash Lawn-Highland, but I was singing well. I was fortunate enough to receive a contract with Ash Lawn, in fact, to sing Papagena and the Second Lady and to cover Pamina in Mozart's *The Magic Flute*. I returned to my ENT for my one-month follow-up appointment with confidence. This time, the doctor, a well-known columnist, told me that I had a water cyst on one of my vocal cords. It probably wouldn't be a problem, he said, but if I wasn't happy with my sound at the extreme top (my "money" notes), I might want to consider having it surgically removed.

Of course, my high notes vanished overnight, and I began to cry through every lesson. I was about to graduate with no boyfriend, no job, and, worst of all, no voice. I was able to get through my role that last semester, Despina in Mozart's *Così fan tutte*, because it was relatively low for me. My voice teacher eventually encouraged me to get a second opinion about the cyst. This second doctor told me that water cysts come and go all the time, he didn't see anything on my cords, and he never would have mentioned it to me even if he had seen a cyst. My high notes promptly returned.

In the meantime, I had been crying through all of my lessons because I was afraid to sing and reinjure myself. Miss Faull insisted that I talk to a counselor, but I told her I couldn't afford one on my own. Literally the next day, I saw a notice on the music stand in the Curtis lobby, where important items were always posted: "Having trouble now that the holidays are over? Come talk to me about it. Free for Curtis students and confidential." I called the number and discovered that Curtis covered this service. Dr. Maggio helped me to realize that I based my entire concept of my self-worth on my singing. Over time she guided me into a slightly more inclusive approach to my self-esteem.

I found my third therapist in the great city of New York. A cab driver once told me that when you live in New York, your age should be calculated in multiples the same way it is for dogs and cats—you live five years for each year you spend there. I was lonely and unhappy; being a native New Yorker only helped in minor ways, especially since my family no longer lived there. I was temping at American Express, I wasn't singing as much as I wanted to, and I wasn't teaching anywhere. I knew I had not found the life I wanted to have. My new therapist, Estelle, was a diminutive Jewish mother, and I warmed to her immediately. At the end of the first session she told me her fee, and I began to cry, saying I wouldn't be able to come back. She smiled, shrugged her shoulders, and said, "What are you gonna do? We're married now." Then she let me pay her what I would have paid if I'd had insurance. This arrangement continued for almost two years. During that time I explored the reasons for my career decisions with her gentle guidance. She was the one who helped me realize that I was pursuing an operatic career because I thought I had to, when what I really wanted to do was teach. At this writing it has been nine years since I left New York, and I still send her a card every December at the holidays. I always receive a long letter in response, commenting on what I told her and asking probing questions about any area I avoided.

My most recent foray into therapy began as the direct result of a painful experience at my first full-time college teaching position. Prior to that I had spent three sheltered years as a graduate assistant at Florida State University. During the final year, I worked with the wonderful tenor Stanford Olsen, teaching his studio for about half the year while he was in and out of town performing. I was still bright-eyed and bushy-tailed when I arrived at Howard Payne University, my first full-time university position. At the interview I had been asked how I would feel about living in such a small town. It never occurred to me that the small town might not accept me, and I was naïve about my permanent status as an outsider. Professionally it was a successful year, but personally it was much harder than I could have expected. What happened there cost me my innocence as a teacher, and my recovery was difficult, even when I landed a much more important position at the University of North Texas.

By this time, however, I knew I didn't have to be ashamed to seek professional help. For me, therapy has been an ongoing process of managing depression, coping with stressful events, and finding new ways to know myself. I have learned that I have to deal with things as they come without repressing anything or lying to myself about anything, particularly if I want to keep authenticity in my work. I have accepted the fact that this profession carries its own set of issues, and it requires me to be unsparing in my self-knowledge.

Artists and Depression

Many writers have acknowledged that artists experience depression more frequently and perhaps more intensely than members of the general population. The stereotypical reasons for this include sensitivity to life's injustices, self-involvement, and a distorted perspective of the world. I think musicians have a more intense way of looking at life, and I think our art is a correspondingly intense way to express our feelings. Singers experience this to a particularly potent degree because our bodies are the instruments. We sing the words, and we feel the complexity of emotions resounding within our very bodies. How could we remain unaffected emotionally?

Singers have a whole host of issues unique to their profession, beginning with the obvious ambiguities in dealing with text. Sometimes the text we are given is far more exposed than we would personally choose to be, and this creates emotional difficulties. The constant worries about vocal health and function can be incapacitating at times. Because we tend to confuse the voice with ourselves, we are disproportionately upset when our voices malfunction. Some singers talk about feeling as if they are under a cloud when they are unable to sing. During the course of the illness, they feel as though they are not truly whole, or as though they will never be able to sing again. Dealing with criticism from family, friends, and strangers about every aspect of their presentation can present additional psychological issues for the singer.

One other issue separates all musicians from all non-musicians: the idea that talent itself isolates them from other people to a certain extent. Many musicians choose to spend their lives with other musicians, and whether or not that is by conscious choice, they say that they feel a bond with musicians unlike any other. There have been many times in my life when I have suddenly felt like a circus freak in a group of non-musicians as they question me about my voice. It is extremely difficult for non-musicians to understand the passion musicians feel for their work. Singers have a harder time here as well because many instrumentalists don't have an appreciation of the particular emotional issues that come with the voice, leaving the singer with an even smaller pool of potentially sympathetic companions.

Ultimately, every person deserves to be happy, and singers are no exception. I have had students over the years with sizeable emotional problems, and it is not always clear how it is most appropriate for me to help. I usually start by finding a way to assure them that I care much more about their developing into healthy, well-adjusted human beings than I do about whether they sing well. Many universities have counseling services available free of charge, and I often encourage students in trouble to avail themselves of them. Many of the students are covered by some sort of health insurance as well, usually through their parents, and I have occasionally helped them find a sympathetic ear.

Even in this advanced age, some students see therapy as a sign of weakness or even lack of faith in God. During my year at Howard Payne University, one of my students told me in unambiguous terms that she wanted to commit suicide. When I discovered that Howard Payne did not have a psychological counseling program, I sent an e-mail to the university's president. He returned my e-mail with a phone call, during which he explained that Howard Payne was not legally required to provide such a program. He recommended that I encourage the student to confess to her minister. What exactly she had done wrong was unclear to me. Given her circumstances, I knew that this student would not share all of the details with her minister. Part of her depression stemmed from her guilt over knowing her minister would not approve of her choices. I felt utterly helpless. She withdrew from school a few weeks later, and I don't know how things turned out for her.

The Teacher's Role

I see my role as the person who identifies a student in distress, evaluates the impact it has on their studies, and guides them to professionals when the problems fall outside my area of training. Most voice teachers joke about the percentage of time we function as therapists. I usually point out that psychiatrists and psychologists are paid a lot more per hour than we are. It is impossible to ignore the student's personality and emotional make-up when we are trying to develop whole artists. Sometimes that means the student will be happier in a different area of the profession. Occasionally it means putting that student's personal health before their vocal studies.

During my second fall semester at Florida State, one of my favorite students returned with a completely different personal affect. Katie* had been a cheerful, happy-go-lucky freshman, but she now cried almost every week at her lesson, and she was virtually unable to sing at all. I knew that she had an older sister who had cancer, and she told me that her sister had died during the summer. I convinced her to visit the school's counseling service, and at that point I could have considered my responsibility to her complete. Things didn't improve in the spring, however, and I decided to talk to our undergraduate advisor. We looked at her grades, which had fallen, and considered the options. I knew I was the only instructor who had one-on-one contact with Katie regularly enough to notice what was happening. The advisor recommended a psychologist in town and asked me to keep him updated on her situation. He agreed that she was at risk and that we needed to be open to whatever decisions would work for her.

Meanwhile, Katie's parents came down from upstate New York and requested a conference with me. Katie signed the necessary confidentiality waiver, and we arranged a meeting. As soon as her parents saw me, they stopped dead and looked at each other with surprise. Apparently I physically resembled the older daughter to an astonishing degree, a fact that Katie had not shared with them or with me. Now I knew why she had been ambivalent about her studies with me even as she attached herself to me as a substitute. Her parents also explained that the older sister had been incapacitated at their home for the last three years, and it had been difficult for Katie to be so far away. Eventually we decided as a team, along with Katie, that it would be best for her to transfer to a music education program closer to home, which she then did.

Not every situation requires this level of attention, and it is advantageous for teachers (and singers) to have simpler solutions on hand. Bookstores are teeming with self-help books, but at this writing not many of them are either significantly helpful or relevant to singers' issues in particular. I recommend two general books to students just beginning to explore the personal issues that affect their voices. *Feeling Good: The New Mood Therapy* (David Burns, M.D.)[1] may help the student assess his or her level of emotional difficulty and determine whether therapy would be helpful. Written for the average reader, this book presents cognitive therapy in layman's terms. Dr. Burns believes that our thought processes cause our emotional problems and that we can learn to change those thoughts. The book is especially helpful for students with milder difficulties.

Another general book, *Emotional Alchemy: How the Mind Can Heal the Heart* (Tara Bennett-Goleman)[2], helped me a great deal. I personally found that Dr. Burns' book covered concepts with which I was already familiar, and I needed a fresh perspective. This book deals with similar issues of emotional patterns, but the writing is less aggressively positive, and it acknowledges the difficulty of actually changing lifelong patterns. Bennett-Goleman explores typical ways in which these patterns are formed, basing her solutions on Buddhist principles. Her method does not ask the reader to simply replace negative thoughts. The Buddhists suggest that the first step to removing these thoughts is to become aware of them and to try to remain an observer in that awareness. By recognizing negative patterns when they occur, we can gain necessary emotional distance, which helps us begin to defuse the intensity of the emotional reaction.

For conflicting emotions about being a singer, Julia Cameron's book *The Artist's Way*[3] can help students consider their reasons for the paths they have chosen. This twelve-week course guides the reader through different obstacles faced by many artists, including misconceptions about creative people, people in our lives who make us feel diminished, and competition. Cameron conceived the course following her series of sessions with blocked writers, but her ideas are relevant to anyone pursuing the creative life. For many of my students, merely thinking of themselves as "artists" (as opposed to technical singers) invites an entirely new dynamic.

Finally, I must recommend the works of James Jordan, to which this book owes its very existence. *The Musician's Soul* purports that ensemble directors must accept and love both themselves and the group to create an atmosphere in which art can grow. Everyone in the room must trust that they are safe before they can feel free to make mistakes. When these mistakes happen, conductors and teachers must avoid the trap of becoming angry and finding a scapegoat. The results will be infinitely more honest and beautiful when everyone is accepted in a human way.

> If one believes that music is self-expression, then it should follow that one must have a self to express. Before one is able to conduct and evoke artistry from singers, one must spend a considerable amount of time on oneself, on one's inside self.[4]

Jordan has recently written a sequel entitled *The Musician's Spirit.*[5]

The ideas discussed in this chapter surely would have been dismissed as nonsense years ago. Many present day teachers believe that it is impossible to deal with students personally and continue to maintain high musical standards. I contend that students rise to standards far beyond my imagination when I believe in them as human beings and enable them to do the same. I have seen the results many times and been both amazed and proud. In our post-September 11 age, we must continue to search for humane ways to treat both others and ourselves.

Notes

1. David Burns, *Feeling Good: The New Mood Therapy* (New York: William Morrow, 1989).

2. Tara Bennett-Goleman, *Emotional Alchemy: How the Mind Can Heal the Heart* (New York: Harmony Books, 2001).

3. Julia Cameron, *The Artist's Way: A Spiritual Path to Higher Creativity* (New York: G.P. Putnam's Sons, 1992).

4. James Jordan, *The Musician's Soul* (Chicago: GIA Publications, Inc., 1998), 9.

5. James Jordan, *The Musician's Spirit* (Chicago: GIA Publications, Inc., 2002).

5

Chapter Five: Perception of Singers

"Born with a Voice," "Illiterate," "Neurotic"

When I talk about my career to strangers on airplanes, they often ask me how I can get up in front of all of those people. What, indeed, does it take for singers to summon the requisite strength to open their mouth onstage in this rare, antiquated art form? The most obvious answer is that one has to believe one has something special to offer, something that no other singer has. We must believe our talents are unique or we will not be able to walk out onto the stage. Most normal people are not asked to bare themselves regularly in this way, and, consequently, they have little understanding of the function of ego in a performer's life.

Most people are not subject to criticism of their work by the public at large, either. Singers seem to carry an extra burden here, professional reviews aside. The average person is not likely to comment on a concert violinist's technique, but even the least trained observer will offer judgments on numerous aspects of a singer's performance, including personal appearance and demeanor. I can remember a terrible argument I had with a non-musician relative who told me at the dinner table that my German was impeccable but my Italian was "lousy." In the eyes of my family, my reaction was perhaps too sensitive. But the public nature of what we do opens us up to such free commentary. No one would have considered a critique of my brother's work as a manufacturing engineer for Motorola to be appropriate dinner conversation, largely because we all knew that we understood little of what he actually did. Many people think they do understand something of what it is to be a singer, and, therefore, respect and distance are not required. After all, everyone can sing; it's not like we had to study for years in order to play our instrument. You can either sing, or you can't, right?

It seems to be generally accepted knowledge that music is not a lucrative profession. I once heard a radio commercial in which a mother tries to tell her eighteen-year-old son that "a career in music probably isn't going to work out." For the average person, a career in music means playing with a band performing some form of popular music. For most professional classical musicians, supporting themselves involves ensemble work (orchestra or wind symphony), often supplemented by teaching. Though there are many professional choral groups in this country, almost none of them pays enough to constitute a singer's entire living.

Many people would not find this hard to believe because it is a common belief that no real training is required to sing. You are born with a voice, or you are not. This perception grew following a 1984 production of Puccini's *La bohème* starring country singers Linda Ronstadt and Gary Morris. The negative reviews did nothing to dispel the notion that popular singers could sing opera without any additional training. Today's spate of "crossover" singers successfully marketing themselves as "opera" singers (Andrea Boccelli, Russell Watson, Summer, and Josh Groban, to name a few) shows that the trend continues. The phenomenal success of Charlotte Church has led countless young sopranos to attempt repertoire far beyond their abilities.

The advent of *American Idol* and all of its imitators has only served to spread the idea that no singing lessons are necessary, that it's perfectly acceptable (and even humorous) to make rude comments about any singer's performance, and that the only real money (and, therefore, validity) is in popular music. Non-musicians ask me all the time if I watch the program. In my profession I'm required to sit through days on end of vocal auditions, and the last thing I want to do when I get home at night is witness the whole process being turned into a sideshow. My students have learned to tease me by threatening to go to the regional *Idol* auditions, or by mock raving about the latest *Idol* winner's new album.

The world of professional classical singers is small and insular, making it unlikely that most average people know even one. In my life, I repeatedly have felt like something of a zoo animal when people learn that I sing opera. They ask dozens of questions about what I do and what it's like to perform in these situations. The conversation almost always ends with the person telling me how lucky I am to make a living at something I truly love.

Within the world of professional musicians, stereotypes about singers abound. Many instrumentalists see us as illiterate trained seals, despite the fact that we are required to communicate and interact in several foreign languages. (I was once told at a job interview at a music high school that I was "dangerously literate for a singer.") On the contrary, an inability to master the language work halts the careers of many young singers. Some words used to describe singers include neurotic, self-centered, non-musicians, flamboyant, fat, glamorous, hypochondriac, *divas*, starved for attention, loud, aggressive, overconfident, overdressed, and chosen on the basis of appearance rather than talent. It is equally difficult when you fit these labels as it is when you don't. Some of them are career expectations, particularly anything involving presentation. For example, the introduction to John Moriarty's famous book, *Diction*, has the following opening sentence: "The American singer who desires a career in opera has to be able to act, perhaps dance, look like a movie star, and sing expertly in at least four languages."[1] With these requirements, it is surprising that anyone chooses this field.

The truth is that many singers are louder (more "vocal"), more flamboyant, more hypochondriacal, and more likely to pay attention to their appearance than other types of musicians. The growing frequency of televised operas gives opera directors even more reason to cast heavily on the basis of appearance. Many musical theater directors have begun to venture into opera directing, as competition for similar positions in theater has increased. A musical theater director is highly likely to weigh appearance more significantly than a conductor would in listening to the same audition.

Recently an international media scandal erupted when renowned soprano Deborah Voigt was fired from a scheduled Royal Opera at Covent Garden production of *Ariadne auf Naxos* by Richard Strauss because she couldn't fit into a black cocktail dress. The casting director had changed the concept of the production, and Ariadne (Voigt's signature role) would wear the said black dress instead of the usual toga. An editorial in the New York Times explained:

> Opera fans are used to extending their senses beyond seeing a body on the stage, which is but one piece in a pageant. It's the musicality that matters. But as audiences are graying, opera houses are looking for ways to pack in a younger crowd. Casting directors trying to make opera hip may be turned off by "big hips," like those Ms. Voigt admits to owning. In this case, the decision will deny British audiences an opportunity to hear and see a performer who may be at the peak of her powers.[2]

One can only hope that the subsequent public outrage was virulent enough to prevent this type of casting decision from becoming the norm.

The idea that singers are more neurotic than other musicians makes complete sense to me, as we are alone in dealing with the reality of actually being our own instruments. It is difficult to imagine an orchestra member losing a job because of his or her appearance, yet it happens to singers every day. Appearance matters in all fields to some degree, but the singer is almost always the person out front taking the hits, in both classical and popular styles. It still smarts for me to recall the day my new teacher casually asked me during the warm-ups if I'd ever considered having my nose done. "You've noticed, haven't you? There's a little too much on the end, and it's just not attractive from all angles. You'll have to consider the photos." Somehow I doubt that these comments would be considered appropriate during the average string player's lesson.

How Singers' Egos Are Affected

Singers who are not naturally extroverted people face a difficult path for many reasons. They often suffer from a lack of confidence in large groups of singers, and they may not receive as much attention from conductors and directors. It can be more stressful for them to manage rehearsals and performances. They may resent being viewed with disdain by the orchestra members just because they are singers. No one is more easily distrusted or disliked in a group of singers than a singer who is not only the best vocalist, but who is a warm, supportive person. In my experience, the most genuinely talented singers tend to be the ones who don't feel the need to exalt themselves over others. As one of the characters in Arthur Miller's play *Death of a Salesman* notes, "He don't have to [talk about it]. He's gonna do it."[3]

In the opera world, stereotypes extend to each voice category. Years ago, I saw a cartoon illustrating what each voice type thinks about while singing. The soprano pictures the curtain calls (with flowers), the mezzo-soprano thinks about the baritone, the tenor counts the money, the baritone imagines a diagram of the resonance in his head, and the bass sees himself fishing. Most singers find the cartoon amusing because it plays into our common perceptions about each voice type. Tenors are considered to be particularly vapid, second only to sopranos. "Soprano jokes" abound; one of my personal favorites gives multiple answers to the question "How many sopranos does it take to screw in a lightbulb?"

- Three: one to do it, one to knock the chair out from under her, and one to say, "I told you it was too high for you, dear."

- None: her accompanist does it for her.

For sopranos, things are especially tough, and not just because there are so many more of them around than any other voice type. Her roles are often expected to carry the evening, yet she faces resentment from mezzo-sopranos in smaller roles. A whole category of roles exists in the *bel canto* repertoire known as *che dici?* roles. These mezzos play nurses or confidantes whose function is to ask *Che dici?* (What are you saying?), allowing the soprano to explore her emotions in an extended aria. While mezzos and baritones less often take the leading role, the subsequent pressure on them is sometimes less intense. Mezzos are often viewed as sexier and less neurotic than sopranos. Tenors are considered to be less virile than baritones, a stereotype happily embraced by many baritones. One joke explains, "The tenor gets the soprano onstage, but it's the baritone who goes home with her after the rehearsal." There is a particular mystique attached to every voice type.

Teaching Other Ways

As a singer and teacher, I have searched for ways to live with these stereotypes without capitulating to them. I have always believed that it is possible to have a career in music even if you are not easily classified into these types. This is true for personality types more than for vocal types. Singers who fit squarely into the center of a vocal category and look like the characters whose roles they sing have a much easier time starting their careers. This is one of the paradoxes of the opera singer's life: how to conform to the expectations of the role category while maintaining an independent personality. Conforming too completely to the norm will get a singer an apprenticeship (i.e., chorus role) but will be a hindrance to moving up to the soloist level.

One of my most advanced students at this writing is a talented young baritone. Trent* entered my studio as a music education major whose primary instrument was trumpet. At the time, he was twenty-seven years old and pursuing a "second" bachelors degree after nearly completing a degree in engineering at another university. He was over six feet tall, strikingly good-looking, and had a raw instrument, everything needed to become an opera singer. However, he was not a diligent student. Eventually I told him that if he really wanted to be a high school band teacher, he should buckle down and be a good one. If that was not what he wanted, he could pursue an operatic career. Either way he'd have to start working much harder. Trent continued to slack off, and at the end of the semester I told him that he could no longer be a member of my studio, that it was not fair to the other students for me to lower my standard for him simply because of his talent. Trent begged me to give him another chance, and I relented, allowing him to register for the spring semester.

In January he auditioned for our undergraduate performance degree. Because he had been at the University of North Texas for several years before I arrived, and his work habits had been nothing if not consistent, the faculty hesitated. One person said that he would never amount to anything. I admitted that while she may turn out to be right, he had the voice and the look, and we should give him a chance. Not long after that, he auditioned for the opera department, and the rest, as they say, is history. He went on to perform leading roles in many of North Texas' productions and then to complete two apprenticeships with professional opera companies. His future is still uncertain, even with all of his gifts, and only time will tell if he has the drive and the luck necessary to make a career.

Trent is relevant to this discussion because the very things that define him may hold him back if he is not careful. Born and raised in Fort Worth, Texas, he is a country boy through and through. His outside interests include NASCAR races, hunting, and fishing, all of which take a distant second to the wife and baby son he adores. His family supports his career choice even though they don't have a frame of reference for it. Trent is a teddy bear completely without artifice or cynicism. He loves with his whole heart, and he knows nothing of Northeast condescension. These qualities, I believe, contribute to the sheer beauty of his voice and to the naked honesty of his singing (particularly in American repertoire), the two most distinctive aspects of his singing talent. I worry about what will happen to him when he finds himself in a more secular, cutthroat world than the one he has grown up to expect. His early years of low expectations have sapped his confidence and delayed his career entry.

Anthony Storr refers to creative talent as a "Janus-faced endowment": "Those who possess it are often regarded with awe and envy because of their gifts. They also tend to be thought of as peculiar."[4] Bookstores and libraries are full of volumes about misunderstood creative souls and the stories of their social isolation. While all creative people are subject to these public misconceptions, singers face a unique brand of stereotyping. Preconceptions about singers can have a devastating effect on the singer's confidence as he or she deals with colleagues, family, and friends.

As a teacher, I try to acknowledge the truths I cannot change about these stereotypes and to validate other choices whenever I can. Certain behaviors are expected of the professional singer: dressing attractively and professionally, managing weight, and interacting with a considerable degree of social confidence and grace. These things are non-negotiable. It helps if you are also extroverted, have a good sense of humor, are unusually attractive, or are intelligent enough to learn your roles but not so intelligent that you either are self-conscious or intimidate the conductor.

That said, singers make their own paths, and I have known many wonderful singers who made their names precisely by being different. While living in New York, I sometimes took my voice lesson immediately following Dawn Upshaw, and our teacher would wish out loud that Dawn would "grow out her hair." It is very difficult for me to imagine Dawn Upshaw with anything other than her trademark short hair, or to think of her career as having followed any traditional path. I try to encourage my singers to be themselves and not to worry too much about whether they "act like singers."

Notes

1. John Moriarty, *Diction* (Boston: E. C. Schirmer Music Company, 1975), xi.
2. *The New York Times* editorial page (March 10, 2004).
3. Arthur Miller, *Death of a Salesman* (New York: Penguin Books, 1983), 95.
4. Anthony Storr, *Solitude: A Return to Self* (New York: Random House, Inc., 1997), ix–x.

Further Exploration

1. Has anyone outside the field of music, a relative or friend, criticized your work in a way that upset you? Describe the incident and your reaction.

_____

_____

_____

_____

2. List adjectives that come to mind when you think of the word "singer."

_____   _____   _____

_____   _____   _____

_____   _____   _____

_____   _____   _____

Go back through the list and put check marks next to the words that describe you.

3. Have you ever been told that your appearance is inadequate for a singer? Describe the experience.

_____

_____

_____

_____

4. List some stereotypes about your particular voice type. Which one is the most distressing to you?

_____

_____

_____

5. Think of five singers you know personally who fit stereotypes about singers (they don't have to be negative stereotypes!) and list those characteristics below.

    1) _____

    2) _____

    3) _____

    4) _____

    5) _____

How do you fit the stereotypes about singers? How are you different?

_____

_____

_____

_____

_____

_____

_____

Chapter Six: Competition and Relationships

When I auditioned for opera apprenticeships in New York, I hated to find out that a friend had gotten an offer because that was too often the way I learned that I had not. The phone calls with offers typically preceded the mailing of the rejection letters. Only one company habitually sent out the letters before they had cast the season. We all joked that they had a pile of the form letters at the auditions and simply signed each one as the day progressed. Normally you knew you still had a chance as long as no one else had received a call. We all had mixed feelings about these calls. We were happy for our friends, but we couldn't deny our own disappointment.

Competition can be one of the most confusing facets of a singer's life. It affects all of our personal relationships, particularly those with other singers. We constantly meet other singers and compare notes on the job, at auditions, and in our social lives. We may have complicated relationships with singers as colleagues, as friends, and sometimes as lovers, all in different ways. It is surprisingly easy to find yourself in a narrow world that includes primarily, if not exclusively, singers and people related to the field. During an opera production, the world seems to shrink even smaller to include only the people involved with the show.

Working with Other Singers

First and foremost, we must deal sensibly with the singers who are our colleagues (unlike our pianist friends who, as solo pianists, never have to deal with anyone). Music is not inherently a competitive sport, but an art form. Yet competition is always present—competition for attention, for roles, for reviews, etc. The smart singer will keep all of that in mind and then compete against him or herself rather than against the other singers in the production or program. Do your best work and it will speak for itself. Anything else is a distraction; if someone else wants to compete with you, they will. Nancy Goldberg, the wise co-director of Belvoir Terrace, advises her staff to "drop the rope" and refuse to be pulled into a dispute. I believe it's good advice for any singer facing a conflict with another singer.

As young singers, we often find ourselves in highly competitive situations before we understand the rules of the game. Some singers thrive on competition and seem to draw strength from constant comparison with others. Other singers may fade into the background, waiting for instruction. By the time they realize what kind of active work is required, it may be too late for them to establish themselves. When programs encompass a wide spectrum of levels (e.g., freshman to doctoral students, or apprentices to international artists), my standard advice to the youngest singers is to observe the interactions of the upper level singers and learn as much as possible about healthy and unhealthy ways of competition.

While I was a student, I enrolled in my first summer program, Nacogdoches Repertory Opera (now defunct) in Texas. At the end of my sophomore year at Bucknell University, I flew out to Texas because I wanted to explore being in an opera, and Bucknell did not have an opera program at the time. The trip was also a consolation prize from my parents because they had not permitted me to transfer to the Eastman School of Music for my junior year. They had said they would allow me to go if I got a scholarship equal to the one I held at Bucknell. I was accepted, and I did receive a scholarship, but it was not comparable. To this day I am grateful to my parents for holding their ground, as I received a top quality liberal arts education and still got accepted into the master's program at the Curtis Institute of Music.

The Nacogdoches program offered two mainstage productions, *La bohème* by Puccini and *The Magic Flute* by Mozart, and a "second-stage" triple bill of *A Hand of Bridge* by Barber with *The Old Maid and the Thief* and *The Medium* by Menotti. I was cast as Laetitia in *Old Maid*, First Spirit in *The Magic Flute*, and children's chorus in *La bohème*, as I was one of the youngest students in the program. My suitemates were both older. Maria*, a graduate student at the Juilliard School in New York, and Joanna*, a statuesque blonde from the Jerome Hines School in New Jersey, were cast in *La bohème* as Mimi and Musetta, respectively. I learned a great deal from those two talented ladies that summer, especially from Joanna's situation there.

Joanna was one of three Musettas, and the other two were both students at the school where the program was being held. During the day, we rehearsed scenes in small groups, but the company would assemble every night to rehearse the crowd scene, Act II of *La bohème* (to this day I know every word of that act). The other two Musettas never let Joanna have a chance at staging rehearsals, which infuriated Maria and me. Joanna remained calm, and she practiced the staging every night in her room instead of going out with the group. When it came time to run the act, she drew the third night. This didn't faze her either. The night that Joanna finally took the stage as Musetta was unforgettable. Despite never having walked through the staging with anyone, she knew exactly what she wanted to do. By the end of the act, the director's tongue was literally hanging out of his mouth. That night I decided that this was how I needed to handle any cover (understudy) I ever had, that I would practice on my own and impress everyone with my preparation and skill.

Five years later, I won my first professional job in *The Magic Flute* with the Ash Lawn-Highland Festival in Charlottesville, Virginia, covering Pamina and performing the roles of Papagena and the Second Lady. The production was double-cast, but I was the only cover, and so I never had any rehearsal time as Pamina. One afternoon the soprano singing Pamina announced that she did not want to sing both the run-through the next morning and the *sitzprobe* (orchestra rehearsal) in the afternoon. It was decided that I would sing the morning run. The director was apoplectic, telling the conductor that he would have rehearsed me all along if he'd known this could happen. He held me and one of the baritones singing Papageno for some extra staging. We got almost all of the way through the first act before he dismissed us without a word. I went home and walked through the entire opera again. The other soprano had a much larger voice than mine, but I knew that the role was easier for me because my voice sat higher, and I had something different to bring to the part.

The next morning I felt confident and easy at the run-through. Everyone complimented me at the end, and the director told the conductor that I was "incandescent" (neither the conductor nor the original Pamina attended the morning rehearsal). During lunch, I asked the director why he had been so quiet at our rehearsal the previous night. He said, "Because I knew that faces were going to crack down the middle when they heard you sing this." In the end, I sang one of the orchestra dress rehearsals (singing both of my other roles at the first dress), and eventually I sang three of the actual performances when the first Pamina experienced vocal difficulties.

Of course, things didn't always turn my way. I auditioned twice for the apprentice program at Sarasota Opera and was an "alternate" both times. The first time, I received a call from one of my old college friends. He had been accepted, and he knew that must mean that I had been accepted also. While we were talking, my call waiting rang with another call. It was the director of Sarasota's Apprentice Artist Program calling to tell me that I was an alternate this season. I hated going back to my call with Brian to give him the bad news.

The second time took place a few years later. I was chosen for the callbacks once again and eagerly prepared myself. My friend Kevin "crashed" the auditions (showed up without having sent in an application and asked to be "squeezed in"). This is more feasible for male singers because they are often in short supply. After I sang my second audition, the program's director asked the pianist I had brought with me to come in and speak with him. This time both Kevin and my pianist were offered positions for the season, and I was once again an alternate. My voice teacher called the company to ask what the problem was; they told her I was "the best soprano they heard," but I was "boring." It took me quite a while to let go of that incident.

It can be very difficult for singers to juggle all of the social implications of competition at a program (or in a production). The singers nearly always find themselves vying for the attention of the directors and conductors. Sometimes a singer will lose a friend because she has gotten a coveted role. I usually advise my students not to personalize things. The other singer had the right to audition just as they did, and some people are better than others at separating personal and professional relationships. It is always wise to assume the best about the other person and to give them the benefit of the doubt if they're having difficulties.

I learned this lesson early on as a freshman in high school, just months after my first role in *Man of La Mancha*. This time the role in question was Luisa in *The Fantasticks*, a much bigger, higher role. I didn't think I had a chance because I was only a freshman, and my idol and "big sister" Sarah* was auditioning. Sarah was a senior, and she had sung the leading role of Aldonza in *Man of La Mancha*. After I was cast as Luisa, Sarah never spoke to me again. It was a crushing blow for me at the time. Now that I'm older and presumably wiser, I understand how painful it must have been for her to be left out of the production during her senior year.

One of the trickiest relationships in a singer's life is the competitive friend, the friend who sticks by you as long as you accept that you are less talented (or accomplished, or special) than he or she is. Julia Cameron calls these people "crazymakers":

> Crazymakers are those personalities that create storm centers. They are often charismatic, frequently charming, highly inventive, and powerfully persuasive...everyone around them functions as supporting cast, picking up their cues, their entrances and exits, from the crazymaker's (crazy) whims.[11]

These are people who outwardly seem supportive but have ways of making you feel small and inadequate. You may enjoy this person's company and even have genuine affection for him or her, but you find yourself wanting to make sure you are not around them immediately prior to an important performance (or any other time when you are not feeling confident). It is helpful to identify these people in your life and to protect yourself from their barbs, intended or not. Most of this behavior stems from insecurity, and if you can remember that, you can keep yourself from feeling diminished.

Romantic Relationships between Singers

Romantic relationships between singers can be both extremely tempting and murderously complicated. Two singers are rarely in the same place at the same time on the professional career ladder. The less-talented partner inevitably ends up putting the other one's career first, which can cause resentment in the long-term. For some people, it becomes a way of avoiding their own careers, also a potential problem down the road. Very often one partner has unrealistic ideas about his or her talent, a terribly difficult situation for both people. Aside from all of the aforementioned problems, the amount of travel involved in today's professional operatic career prohibits both partners from performing full-time.

I have been on both sides of this quandary. I have had a major relationship with someone who was more vocally gifted than me, and I have had one in which I was the more accomplished singer. During my years as a master's student at Curtis, I intermittently dated a very talented baritone. David* was a star in the program, and at first I was barely on the radar. I spent quite a bit of time taking care of him: making sure he attended his coachings, feeding him, and teaching him his music, since I was a far superior pianist. All of these activities detracted from my own studies, and I cannot blame him, as the choice was mine. One summer I was offered the role of Norina in Donizetti's *Don Pasquale* at a training program in Belgium. David did not want me to accept the role, as it would mean that I would be out of the country when he returned from his own summer apprenticeship.

I realized that turning down the role would be a mistake, and I had uneasy feelings about what his request meant for our relationship, so I accepted. Before I left for Belgium, I went to visit David at his apprenticeship and found that he was cheating on me with two other singers. A scene ensued, one that was talked about by young singers at Curtis and elsewhere for months afterward.[2] I finally told my teacher about it (at the time I was studying with Ellen Faull at Juilliard) and told her how upset I was that everyone knew. She smiled and said that they wouldn't be talking about me if they didn't think I was a good singer, a "player." Years went by before I understood what she meant.

Oddly enough, I encountered some of the same problems when I dated someone who didn't sing as well as me. He too expected me to give up all career opportunities to be with him. This time I knew better, and I was not about to forfeit worthy projects to tend to someone else's career, particularly when my career was the one flourishing. He clearly didn't want what I wanted, which was a true partnership in which we encouraged each other to pursue our dreams. As of this writing, I am on my own, but, like Zerbinetta, I still believe that one day true love will come along.

Career ambitions affect the singer's family life in a variety of ways. For men, this often means asking their wives either to travel with them around the country, putting their own careers on ice, or to stay at home alone with the children while the husband travels. Either scenario can put a strain on the healthiest of marriages. At this writing, I believe it is still more difficult for women to have both a successful career that involves a lot of travel and a committed relationship. Many women manage it, however, with considerable understanding on the parts of their spouses. For physical and practical reasons, these women may postpone, or forgo entirely, having children.

Voice Competitions

No discussion on competition would be complete without a consideration of formal voice competitions. At Curtis we were often told not to bother with them unless we had good reason to think we could win substantial prize money. Competitions involved a limited number of singers (and the results were therefore less meaningful), the judging was always political, the application fees were exploitative, and they would rarely, if ever, lead to any actual professional work. While I was a student there, I watched a group of singers spend a year going through various rounds of an international competition. During the final round, an entire afternoon of singers was essentially discounted because the famous singer (for whom the competition was named) spent that time signing autographs at the Museum of Art instead of listening to them. Ironically, the winners of this competition actually did receive work with the Opera Company. Singers in Philadelphia would later lament having lost a job to a "Wiener." The term came about because the famous singer often chose as many as forty winners, announcing in his Italian accent that "we are all *weeners* here!"

My personal experience with competitions has borne out the Curtis rule of thumb. I didn't compete in very many of them when I was a full-time singer, although I was twice a semifinalist in the New York Oratorio Society Competition. As a doctoral student at Florida State, I participated in the Suncoast Opera Guild Competition for the sole reason that I needed the money. I had been there with a student the year before and realized that the money was there for the taking. When they announced that I had won first place (and $2,500), all I could think was: "Now I'll be able to pay all of my fees and graduate!"

In the final round of the competition, we chose numbers from one to ten to determine the order in which we would sing. I drew number one and assumed it was over for me, since the judges would inevitably leave scoring room for later singers. After I sang, I learned that singer number two had switched places with singer number seven because she'd been planning to sing the same aria I had, "Regnava nel silenzio" from Donizetti's *Lucia di Lammermoor*. At the time, I was thirty-two years old, and the poor young thing cowering alone in the corner couldn't have been more than twenty-one, so the teacher in me decided to go over and talk to her.

I smiled as I approached her and apologized for singing her aria. Wide-eyed, she told me I'd sung it beautifully and said she was thinking about singing something else. She was clearly in a state of panic. I told her she should sing the piece she felt best about, that it might be a mistake to sing something she hadn't prepared. She was relieved because it turned out that she didn't really have anything else. She was an undergraduate thinking about pursuing a master's degree at Florida State, and we had a nice conversation about my teacher there. She was much calmer after we finished talking.

When I returned to the group of Florida State singers and pianists (there were two others in the finals), they all wanted to know why I was talking to the competition. "What did you do that for?" one person said. "She's singing your aria." "Look at her," I said. "She's a lot younger than I am, she's scared to death, and the chances that she is really ready to sing Lucia are slim to none." Besides, I had already sung, and the judges were going to pick the voice they liked the best anyway. Ensuring that another singer had a bad experience wasn't going to make me a better singer. When the young singer sang the "Regnava," it was clear that she had a lovely voice, but the aria was a little beyond her maturity level. The teacher in me, though, cheered for her for holding her ground and getting through it as well as she had. I was almost happier about that than I was about my own performance, yet another indication that teaching is where I belong. (Of course, I was still happy that I won the first prize.)

In talking with my students about voice competitions, I am very cautious about which ones I advise them to enter. My university is actively involved in the regional NATS auditions, so my students usually participate in those. Before they go, I remind them to sing for themselves, for the experience of singing; if they place, that's icing on the cake. Like any other competition, the judging is uneven, and I don't want any of my students to be unduly heartbroken. They learn a great deal from the experience, even when the comments and scores lack justification.

Most classical singers have a certain degree of natural competitive spirit stemming from their joy in their own sounds. Responsible teachers encourage this spirit of confidence in the individual students without comparing them unfavorably to each other. Each student should feel that his or her product is "worthy of competition in his class" (as the NATS statement reads). There is no benefit to the belief that you must always be the best one in the room. No one wants to work alongside someone who needs to put others at a disadvantage in order to feel comfortable. The fact remains that you will not always actually *be* the best one in the room, and that form of confidence can quickly evaporate with nothing to replace it. There will also be many situations in which you may perhaps be the best singer, but the judges select someone else; it can be difficult to manage the resulting anger. I have always believed that it is best to know you are worthy of competition because no one else has your voice, your set of life experiences, and your way of singing. You cannot control what others will think, but you *can* control how you view yourself.

Notes

1. Julia Cameron, *The Artist's Way* (New York: G. P. Putnam's Sons, 1992), 44–45.
2. I considered changing my flight to one several days earlier but eventually decided to stick it out. On the afternoon of the earlier flight not taken, I was watching TV only to learn that the flight had crashed in Sioux City, Iowa. My young, romantic heart took this as a "sign" that David and I were supposed to be together, of course, and I stayed with him for four more disastrous months.

Further Exploration

1. Can you recall a time when you were in direct competition with a friend for a singing role or solo and lost to your friend? How did the incident affect the way you felt about yourself? About your friend?

_____

_____

_____

_____

2. What is the most important lesson you have learned about competition from observing the behavior of an older singer? (It can be a positive lesson or a lesson in "what not to do.")

_____

_____

_____

3. If you have ever lost a friend over a role or prize, take a moment to mentally forgive him or her and/or yourself. Let go of the negative feelings. Give thanks for the good times you were able to have with that person, and wish them well in their lives. Clear the slate for the next time you see them.

4. What do you think drives the "crazymakers" in your life to put you or other people down?

_____

_____

Think about how you will tactfully deflect the barbs the next time they come. Plan "safe times" to enjoy this person's company and times when you will want to be with people who are better able to support you.

5. Have you ever dated a singer? _____
   How did the difference in talent or career levels affect your own singing? (The answer can be both positive and negative.)

   _____

   _____

   _____

   _____

   _____

6. In the voice competitions you have entered, did you generally feel that the judging was fair and appropriate?

   _____

   _____

   What would you tell a singer about to enter his or her first voice competition?

   _____

   _____

   _____

   _____

Chapter Seven: Academia

Academia is a tough place to be a singer. The "ivory tower" image, in which professors sit in isolated places discussing ideas that have no bearing on the everyday life, carries over into music schools to some degree as well. In most major music programs, faculty members are required to stay active within the field, which typically entails continued performance of some kind. Nevertheless, it can be very difficult to stay abreast of hiring trends in the operatic world when you are ensconced in a miniature society with its own set of aesthetic standards. It is also hard to balance your investment in your own singing/academic career with the future of your students, particularly if you have unresolved ego issues of your own. Our willingness to prioritize the students' needs affects every area of our interaction with them, from repertoire decisions, to auditions, to handling their failures. For students, this is a critical stage of development, and they may have little information with which to determine whether they are on the optimal path.

Dealing with Repertoire Issues

No area is as critical to a voice student's success, or is as difficult for the teacher to negotiate, as the issue of repertoire. To develop a sense of our own musical temperament, we inevitably begin by experimenting with many different styles and by immersing ourselves in wider repertoire. Our teachers assign pieces to us, generally covering a wide range of emotional and musical territory. Often we are told that it is irrelevant whether we relate to a particular piece: we will sing it because it is required. If the teacher is knowledgeable, the piece will be appropriate for our age and level of vocal training. To a certain point, this approach has merit. There is a canon of basic repertoire with which all singers should be familiar. Some songs make particularly good teaching pieces because they present fundamental technical issues within a manageable artistic framework.

I try to tailor my students' repertoire to meet their needs, both vocally and artistically, from the very beginning of their studies. I do not believe it is ever too early to begin the process of artistic communication. I usually assign several pieces and ask them to choose the one that holds the most meaning for them. Schubert wrote so many wonderful *Lieder*, for example, that the student might as well make his own selection (from my own strategically chosen group). In this way, they become familiar with several pieces instead of just one, and they begin to develop a sense of what they should look for in prospective repertoire. Occasionally students come to me and say that they really hate a song and want to change it. If I'm confident that they're not trying to camouflage a lack of preparation, I agree, telling them that there are too many great songs in the world to sing one that they hate. I make sure that the replacement piece has similar technical and musical demands.

When a singer is not comfortable with the material, he or she will be unable to communicate anything clearly to the audience. It is vital to begin the process of learning to communicate with a piece that capitalizes on the singer's natural personality. Most singers are much more likely to involve themselves in their performances when they relate to the emotional content of the text. I believe that this is just as big a concern when choosing art song repertoire as it is in opera. Beginning with a piece that utilizes the singer's temperament will surely be more successful than attempting a less familiar character, or as I call it, starting behind the proverbial eight ball.

As singers learn more of the repertoire, they can identify works and composers with whom they feel a natural affinity. It is important not to limit oneself too early, but to continue expanding the base of comfortable repertoire. As we become more secure within our natural framework, we can move outward into more adventurous texts, as opposed to beginning with works for which we are ill-equipped and whittling the list down to a manageable few. A young singer will have a better chance with the piece technically if the musical/dramatic component is not also a difficult variable.

Nowhere is this truer than in opera. As young singers, we want to sing everything, and we may not understand the long-term effects of making unreasonable demands on our instruments. Many teachers believe that it is never too early to begin studying roles that will perhaps be more appropriate later in our careers. While this may sound like a good idea on paper, it can be dangerous in practice. Too often, the student then listens to recordings of much more mature singers and attempts to imitate their performances. These students manufacture a sound that is unnatural to their youthful instruments while trying to add years to the process overnight. This may be successful initially, but the student can only work against the natural function of the instrument for a limited time before problems develop. Of course, by this time the production or competition in question may be over, with both student and teacher having received accolades accompanied by statements of disbelief that the student is "only X years old."

My own vocal experience has led me to believe that muscle memory is a tenacious thing. Therefore, it may be better for students, particularly undergraduates, to cut their teeth on repertoire they are able to sing now but may be considered "baby repertoire" later in their careers. When I auditioned for the master's program at Curtis at the age of twenty-one, I offered Norina's aria from *Don Pasquale* by Donizetti, Aennchen's aria "Kommt ein schlanker Bursch gegangen" from *Der Freischütz* by Weber and "Monica's Waltz" from *The Medium* by Menotti. Only one of these arias, Norina, is an adult role from an opera that is frequently performed. The top range in Norina's aria proved to the audition panel that I had the vocal material for the program; it was necessary for me to have at least one piece that demonstrated this ability. Yet I have been plagued in later life by my early muscle memory in this aria. I have sung the complete role of Norina several times, and the aria feels completely different to me than the rest of the role. If my entire undergraduate diet had consisted of this type of standard piece, I would have been saddled with a teenager's vocal problems in many of the roles I later sang professionally. (I never did sing either the Aennchen or the Monica again after that audition, either in the role or as an audition aria, having moved on to more "grown-up" arias once I started at Curtis.)

Consider that we are talking about Donizetti, whose works (with the exception of *Lucia di Lammermoor* and a few others) suit young voices very well. Mozart, Rossini, Handel, and Donizetti are the staples for professional singers in their twenties. Yet it is not uncommon to hear undergraduate singers perform arias and duets by Verdi, Puccini, Cilea, and various *verismo* composers. These singers may be able to get through these works temporarily, but the long-term damage to their careers is impossible to calculate. It is the teacher's responsibility to serve as an advocate for the student, to veto any role or aria that may not be in their best interests. The teacher must have the confidence to say "no" when saying "yes" might boost his own reputation.

When a student flounders for any reason, it is even more critical that the teacher be supportive. Again, this seems to be an issue of confidence. The teacher may only be able to see how the student's poor performance reflects on him, rather than considering what kind of teaching the student will need from him to get back on track. At this point, some teachers wash their hands of the student, telling colleagues that the student doesn't work hard, or is "difficult," or is sick all of the time. Sometimes these conditions are indeed true. It can be hard to see a relationship with a student through, to continue to be available when they are no longer productive members of the studio (sometimes because they have graduated). There are certainly circumstances under which a student should be removed from the studio. But when a student experiences vocal problems, our help is needed even more. We then need to consider what we should change about the student's repertoire or technique or whether the student should be counseled into another career. The real work of teaching can be said to occur when we "plant seeds for trees under whose shade we do not expect to sit."

Occasionally a student has trouble because we have assigned a piece that is inappropriate for some reason. Often we realize this at some point during a lesson, and we need to be honest with the student about it. Recently, I spoke at a teachers conference in San Antonio, and one of the teachers asked me how I handled it when I realized I had given a student an inordinately challenging piece and the piece was already scheduled for "contest." First, I hope to realize it before it's too late to change it. Second, I simply tell the student that I've made an error ("teacher error," I call it), and we'll need to pick something else because the piece didn't go in the direction I thought it would. By the time that happens, I have tried to establish trust with the student, and I believe that being honest increases that trust more than it hurts the student's faith in my abilities.

During the summers, I often work with singers from other areas of the North Texas program. On one such occasion, I worked with a wonderful young jazz singer. Natalie was working on smoothing out her transition between registers, and I'd given her "Pur dicesti" by Lotti in the high key. While she was able to negotiate the leaps up to the high "E," she had a great deal of difficulty staying in the upper part of her voice. I realized that she would have to learn to "turn over" her voice in a more operatic way for that to work, using principles of *aggiustamento*, and this was not a useful goal for her. I explained the situation to Natalie and told her we would discontinue working on the piece. Because I work mostly with classical singers, I told her, it hadn't even occurred to me that the *passaggio* issue would come up, but now that it had, I needed to acknowledge that she shouldn't work with it in this way. She thanked me for recognizing the problem and for explaining the reasons. I told her about the teachers' conference, and she said she was glad I'd been honest with her. Otherwise she just would have thought she wasn't good enough to sing the piece.

The Artist/Teacher: Setting an Example

The artist/teacher of voice has many roles to assume in performing while teaching others to perform. One must protect one's own vocal time and somehow find time to practice among all of the lessons. I find that I have to limit how much demonstrating I do when I have performances on the horizon. Sharing my professional experience with the students when I return, however, can lead to technical breakthroughs for them. I learn new techniques every time I perform because I always have a series of new challenges to solve for myself. What I learn "on the job" often translates into new vocabulary for me as a teacher. I also speak frankly with my students about my performance concerns, from stage fright and dealing with conductors and other singers to contracts and reviews. All of this humanizes me for them and with them.

While I know that an effective teacher must stand somewhat apart from the students (not quite being one of them), I have never seen the benefit of putting myself on a pedestal. I am a singer just as the students are, and though I am further down the career line than they are, I don't have all of the answers because no one does. The "queen bee" dynamic, in which the teacher is the all-knowing arbiter of which students are worthy of praise, has no place in education, let alone music education. I don't want my students to compete for my approval. I want them to do their best work because they respect themselves and the art form enough to do no less. During my first year at North Texas, one of my students was in tears in my office, bemoaning the fact that she couldn't tell "where she stood" in my studio. While I regretted that she was so upset, I was glad that she was unable to determine a ranking system among my students.

I have often had the privilege to perform alongside some of my most talented graduate students in professional situations, sometimes because I recommend them to conductors. I am acutely aware that in these situations the students are looking to me as an example of how to behave. I dress for rehearsals, especially orchestra rehearsals, and I am careful to treat everyone involved with dignity and respect. I have also sung the soprano solos in a number of oratorios at the university, and I try to approach these rehearsals as professionally and collegially as possible. I perform from memory whenever I can, and always for recitals.

Recently my professional ego was tested by a conductor with whom I have worked for years. I sang a role in a Baroque opera with this conductor's New York company. One of the other singers canceled at the last minute, and the conductor asked me if I knew anyone who could learn the role and fit the costume. This was a joint production with a dance company, and he needed someone about my height and weight. I recommended my graduate student Susan*, a beautiful singer and musician who also happens to be a much more innately talented actress than I will ever be. The conductor paid me an additional fee to teach her the role, as he was already out of town. Susan did an outstanding job, and I had the additional pleasure of showing her around New York City. (Her presence during the rehearsal period was a special godsend, as I learned that my father had terminal cancer while we were there. At the time, we were told he had eighteen to thirty-six months. In actual time, we lost him just nine weeks after the diagnosis.)

The company scheduled this production for a revival several years later, only this time Susan was cast (in a different role), and I was replaced by a much younger, much thinner soprano. Worse yet, the conductor didn't tell me himself. I found out when Susan received an e-mail offer and assumed that I had, too. She was very gracious about what could have been an awkward situation. It never occurred to me to be upset or distant with her. I knew that I was a major reason for her success with this conductor, not simply because I had recommended her to him. I was genuinely happy that he liked her work. Of course, it hurt me to be told that I was "wrong" for the production, especially when I wear about the same size as Susan, but my feelings about it had nothing to do with her.

Sometimes setting an example involves turning down roles, for my students as well as for myself. When the North Texas opera department first heard my baritone Trent* (mentioned in Chapter Six), they were interested in casting him as Puccini's *Gianni Schicchi*. I said no because I didn't feel that was a "first role." I also said no to one of my lyric mezzos singing the role of Zita; I said that she could either sing the smaller role of Ciesca or not appear in the production. (Both of these singers eventually held professional apprenticeships.) The following year, our university programmed Beethoven's Ninth Symphony and invited me to sing the soprano solos. I turned it down, and I told my students about it. The soprano who accepted it might not have a big enough voice either, I reasoned, but I would rather have people asking where I was than saying that my voice was too small. I could have gotten through it technically, but the potential cost to my voice was prohibitive because my voice was not the right size or color for the piece.

One of the most important (and least discussed) aspects of setting an example for our students is our behavior toward fellow teaching colleagues. We should not create "cult" studios in which it is understood that we are the only competent teachers on the faculty and these are the only talented students in the program. It is vital to treat other teachers and their students with grace and genuine support. Students pay attention, and they know when we are involved in petty rivalries with other teachers. Using them as pawns in these squabbles belittles us and belittles the students. Conflicts will happen between voice teachers; what is important is the manner in which you deal with them, particularly when students are involved.

Richard Miller describes a particular type of cult teacher as the "technique-mystique teacher":

> Technique becomes a banner that the teacher holds aloft...everything
> that takes place in the studio is part of technical revelation not else-
> where available.[1]

These teachers are detrimental to the health of a voice program and more so to the students who become dependent on them. No one teacher has all of the answers, is right for every type of student, or has a secret lock on all accurate technical information. Miller says, "Students who have been drawn and held by such parochial teachers should begin to ask why the performance world is peopled with successful singers who have not shared in this particular technical wisdom."[2]

A special corner of academia is set aside for the teaching fellow, sometimes called a teaching assistant or graduate assistant. These singers have a difficult road at times. As teachers, they have full grading powers, but they are not faculty; they are students. This distinction is especially confusing for the doctoral students, who tend to be older and more experienced. In some cases, the best doctoral teaching assistants are in fact more effective teachers than some of the faculty members, which creates a potentially awkward situation. Most students return to academia for a doctorate in order to pursue an academic career. Some professors understand that these students will be academic colleagues within a few short years and treat them accordingly. Others see this as a last chance to "haze" the unsuspecting student by emphasizing the menial nature of the job in comparison with being a full faculty member. In advising these doctoral students, I assure them that there are always some faculty members who need to focus on the hierarchy of things. Being "junior faculty" (not yet tenured) comes with its own form of hazing. There are usually only a few who behave in this way, and we must try to surround ourselves with the multitude of good people in academia.

When I first arrived at the University of North Texas, I was happy to find a colleague who also enjoyed Richard Russo's hilarious novel *Straight Man*.[3] Russo's main character is an English professor serving as interim chairman of his department at West Central Pennsylvania University. The novel opens with a search committee meeting during which, among other incidents, the chair is struck in the face with a flying notebook. My colleague, professor of trumpet Keith Johnson, and I agreed that any doctoral students considering a career in academia should read this all-too-accurate satire.

Career Guidance: Staying Current Outside the Bubble

Staying current outside the academic "bubble" takes a great deal of time, but it is absolutely necessary for the serious singer or voice teacher. One must be aware of hiring trends, particularly at the apprentice and regional levels, as they are the next logical step in a graduate student's career. It is not sufficient to follow what is happening at the Metropolitan Opera, as very few people will progress that far, and that usually happens long after the singer leaves academia anyway. Listening to recordings of "hot" young singers can be very helpful, and listening to older recordings must be done with care. Performance practices change throughout the years. What was musically acceptable in the 1950s is very different from what will fly today. It is also important not to listen exclusively to singers in their forties and older. Young singers (in their twenties and younger) do not need to imitate these older, more mature singers, and they cannot do so without considerable long-term damage to their own voices.

During my years in New York City, I spent a lot of my time accompanying in numerous voice studios. This was a great way to be a "fly on the wall" and to observe teachers and singers as though I were invisible. I also spent many hours visiting the lessons of my singer friends, both at Curtis and in Manhattan. We all did this often, and the teachers were (for the most part) open to sharing their ideas with guests. When I returned to academia, I was surprised by how different the priorities were. In general, the repertoire assigned to young singers in academia is much larger than what singers with voices of similar weight sing in conservatories and in the profession.

There are many reasons for this discrepancy, the most benign being casting necessity. Almost any opera chosen by an academic opera department will have "holes," roles that are not generally cast with singers under forty in the professional world, and there are always students who have to compromise. Another reason is that teachers become disenchanted with the basic repertoire and assign repertoire that they are interested in, or that they sang when they were opera singers, even if it is beyond the student's abilities. In academia there are also voice professors who have rarely, if ever, sung on a professional operatic stage, and their concept of the necessary sound may be misguided. In the worst case scenario, teachers assign "large" (Verdi, Puccini, *verismo*, flashy, etc.) arias because they will win competitions, regardless of the inevitable effect on the student's vocal longevity. The most talented students succeed in spite of unrealistic repertoire demands, but many others are sacrificed along the way. One of the saddest days of our faculty year is often the graduate audition day because so many singers have already ruined their instruments by singing inappropriate repertoire.

It is impossible to stay in touch with realistic repertoire without keeping current with the market. One of the best ways to assess the market is to visit apprentice programs and hear the singers who have been hired. Attending performances at regional opera companies can also be informative, as employment with one of these companies often follows a series of apprenticeships. Singers and/or teachers, as well as anyone who has a serious interest in the professional operatic world, must follow the news about up-and-coming singers by listening to CDs, reading reviews, and subscribing to the important trade journals. Currently these include *Classical Singer* and *Opera News*. The *NATS Journal of Singing*, while an excellent source of information, is written primarily for teachers rather than for professional singers. Any career guidance we offer must be based on both the student's long-term success and solid knowledge of the professional market. Most students currently enrolled in voice performance degree programs will not be viable in traditional operatic careers. We must be aware of other options for careers in music and design plans to fit individual student's needs and abilities.

Since I have returned to the university environment, I have noticed the way in which young singers detach themselves from the experience while they are singing. In opera rehearsals, they often seem to be watching other people watch them as the Countess, or as Figaro, as opposed to actually being or doing the role. This phenomenon is even more common in productions of popular *bel canto* and *verismo* standard works, in which stereotypes abound and the students may have no actual emotional context for their roles.

They resort to imitations of famous singers or to approximations of what they think audiences expect to see and hear in these roles. Nothing real or artistically satisfying can ever develop from such a limited personal investment in the material. Yet in many university situations, this sort of manufactured approach to art is encouraged. It is outwardly simpler to imitate someone else than it is to develop one's own interpretation. It takes patience for singers to wait until they have grown vocally and personally enough to handle the role, to have the courage to say no until that time. Sadly, singers who sing their first operatic roles under these circumstances miss the opportunity to create a deeply personal relationship to the art they claim to love.

Ultimately, any singer must acknowledge which love is more compelling to them, the art form of music or the attention and personal glory of being a successful performer. These two loves need not be mutually exclusive. I cannot say I have not enjoyed the applause and kudos that have come with success in the performance world. I do find it disturbing that many singers consider the performance the only important part of the experience, rather than accepting the applause as icing on the cake. Some less confident singers anxiously seek the approval of others following their appearances. I cannot imagine how frightening it would be to rely exclusively on the opinions of others in judging my work. I have always known whether I sang well, long before anyone else offered commentary. My fondest wish for my students is that they will develop inner compasses of their own, so they can integrate the opinions of others without being threatened or controlled by them—and that they will always remember what special people they are, even if they never sing another note.

Notes

1. Richard Miller, *The Structure of Singing* (New York: Schirmer Books, 1986), 211.
2. Ibid.
3. Richard Russo, *Straight Man* (New York: Random House, Inc., 1997).

Further Exploration

1. Name a piece in your repertoire that:
   you don't relate to emotionally. _____
   you feel is beyond you technically._____
   works really well now but didn't
   when you first picked it up. _____
   fits like a glove and always did. _____
   you dropped after working on
   it for a while. _____
   scares you. _____
   makes you happy. _____
   makes you laugh. _____
   you'd like to put away for a while. _____
   you'd like to take out again. _____

2. If you are a student, does your teacher perform regularly?

   _____

   What specific things have you learned from your teacher's example?

   _____

   _____

   _____

   If you are an artist/teacher, do you talk about your performances with your students? What do you most want them to know about your work and what it means to you personally?

   _____

   _____

   _____

3. If you are a student, what do you know about the meaning of collegiality from seeing your teacher with other teachers?

_____

_____

_____

If you are a teacher/conductor, how do you want your students to think of your behavior among your colleagues? Could you set a better example?

_____

_____

_____

If your school has teaching fellows or assistants, would they all speak highly of you upon leaving?

_____

_____

4. What resources do you currently have for staying current with trends in professional hiring?

Journals _____

Performances I can regularly attend _____

_____

_____

Listening _____

_____

Other _____

_____

Chapter Eight: Professional Singing

The worlds of professional singing and academic singing have less in common than one might think. The musical level is often higher in the professional world (but not always) and the exposure is often greater (but not always). In academia, one has the sense that students are practicing for what will take place later, that all mistakes will be forgiven because the singers are students. Perhaps the most profound shock about the professional world is that the clock starts the moment you sing your first job; nothing before that moment counts, and nothing after that moment is forgotten. No professional company cares what roles you sang in school, only that you have sung any roles at all.

The reality of today's opera world demands a thorough understanding of one's temperament. With regard to most of the common voice types, directors cast from such a large pool that singers often joke that they can even find someone with the eye color they have in mind. We must know what characteristics (physical, vocal, and emotional) are normally found in working singers of each voice type so we don't disqualify ourselves from initial consideration. Then we must determine what separates us from the crowd, what we as individuals bring to the material, because it is no longer enough to demonstrate the right generic qualities for your voice type. There are hundreds, if not thousands, of young singers in the field who can negotiate the technical demands of the music. In exploring our talents and weaknesses with a critical eye, we can learn to market ourselves most effectively.

Auditions

Auditions are the first battleground for young singers fresh out of degree programs. Most singers begin with the battery of summer apprentice artist auditions, primarily held in November and December (so the program directors can do their Christmas shopping in New York City). You make the rounds of the usual audition venues, warming up on subway platforms because practice room rentals are costly. You put on your heels (and maybe your whole outfit) in the bathroom because New York is cold and dirty in December. Hopefully the pianist you called will arrive on time, and if you didn't call one, hopefully the company hired someone who knows the arias you are planning to sing.

Dressed and ready, you wait in the hallway, listening to the singers before you. Usually at least one of the other singers is name dropping, talking about an offer she already has, about the director she knows who's in the room, about how they don't want anyone your height, etc. (When I was auditioning, I often hired a certain pianist primarily because he made me laugh while we waited, whispering to me about the fashion mistakes he saw in the room.) To make matters worse, some companies block-schedule singers of the same voice type. On one occasion I found myself in a row of *coloratura* sopranos. The company pianist asked for my piece, and when I gave him "Caro nome," he rolled his eyes and said, "Oh, like I haven't played that today." I smiled as sweetly as I could and said, "Well, you haven't played it with me, have you?" (Even though I didn't get the job, it was satisfying that he botched the introduction and was impressed enough by my singing to be more gracious to me on the way out.)

You survive the waiting room intimidation, and you sing your first aria. Maybe they look up at you while they eat lunch, or maybe they're consumed by their game of "Aria Bingo." Maybe they are absorbed in their paperwork until just before your big high note, and then they lean forward with all of their attention for that one note only. You finish the piece, and you hold your breath, hoping that they'll ask for a second piece. If they don't, you'll know instantly that you didn't get the job. Sometimes they even ask you for a third aria. When they do, you leave that audition with an extra bounce in your step, mentally rewriting the bio you'll send the company for the program.

Then the rejection letter comes, just like the one you got from seven or eight of the other companies, and you start rethinking your career choice. One of my teachers told me she used to paper her bathroom wall with the rejection letters. "All you need is one person to say yes," she said. "The rest don't matter, and you have to be able to forget about them. All you know for sure about auditioning is that if you don't go, you won't get the job." You learn to keep going, to keep creating new options for yourself in the face of constant rejection. One summer my auditions came up empty, so I hired a weekly coach and learned the role of Mozart's Susanna from *Le nozze di Figaro* in Italian, recitatives and all. Eighteen months later when I sang the role, that choice paid for itself.

One cold winter, I attended a workshop on auditioning, with the director Jay Lesenger in New York. At the first class, he asked us what our goal was at the audition. We chimed in easily, "To get the job." "Wrong," he said. "You have no control over that. What you can control is what you are going to communicate about this piece of music on this day." This is invaluable advice for any performer. We never have control over how anyone will react to our work, so it is futile to plan for either a positive or a negative reaction. We can choose one quality we want our listeners to know about this character and focus on communicating that one quality. Not only does it result in more convincing acting, but it is also something positive to think about during the audition.

The Apprenticeship Jungle

Once you land an apprenticeship, you have to focus on getting noticed while you are there. Many singers go through a series of apprenticeships (or just one) and never move up to the next level in the career pyramid. Some of the apprenticeships have as many as forty singers, and if you are not exceptional in some way, you will not be considered for principal roles with that company further down the line. One of the best ways to be noticed is to be prepared. It sounds simple, but many people arrive at these jobs without having every piece thoroughly researched and memorized, expecting the company's coaches to teach them their scene assignments. You must be the one who can save the scene when all others fail, and you will be able to do this because you learned your entrances from the orchestra part. The orchestra is always reliable, while other singers can often be missing in action when things get heated onstage.

Within the group of apprentices, there are typically several "stars," several "mistakes," and a majority of singers who make little or no real impression. There are many ways to become a star, preparation being the first prerequisite. The stars are typically singers who are new on the scene, above average in appearance, and have voices of either unusual beauty or unusual power. Sometimes these singers have prior connections with program staff, and sometimes they don't. Most stars are initially surprised to find themselves thus anointed. Whether they survive depends quite a bit on keeping their egos in check. The very ingenuousness that made them stars can be lost all too quickly, transforming them into *divas* who are then universally hated by the other singers.

The "mistakes" are the singers who have everyone scratching their heads, wondering how they were hired in the first place. Perhaps they had one great audition day, or they provided a voice type badly needed in the program. Sometimes they are last-minute replacements, or simply charity cases on the part of the program director. However they came to be there, these people tend to arrive both under-prepared and ill suited for the performance environment. Often they realize early on that they are in over their heads. They may become defensive and unintentionally further alienate themselves from the rest of the group. Because the opera world is so small, these unfortunate singers have little chance of winning a second apprenticeship with another company.

The singers in the middle ground spend much of their time at the program jockeying for position. There are right ways and wrong ways to go about this. One of the most common mistakes is treating people according to how highly they rank in the company. Some singers are very solicitous of the directors and conductors but may be condescending and dismissive of the coaches and completely above speaking with any of the technical staff. These tactics are blatantly transparent to everyone, and no one appreciates being minimized or ignored. The coaches often have significant input in casting decisions for the following season, particularly in the area of apprenticeship renewals. All of these positions are temporary, also, and it is impossible to know where, or how high up, anyone will be working from year to year.

Young singers should learn immediately that the technical staff members are not "hired help." These professionals are a vital part of every production, and they work long hours to ensure that everything runs smoothly, for little or no personal glory or applause. One summer, I sang an orchestra dress rehearsal of a role I was understudying. The soprano doing the role came backstage (while the costumer was working on my costume) to give me "notes" on all of the things I should have done better, a job that usually belongs solely to the director. A few weeks later, the soprano began having vocal problems and canceled a performance of another role she was singing with the company. The costume department left a message at my residence: "We're already altering the costume for you for Wednesday night!"

Singers who are hired back treat everyone with courtesy, respect, and genuine friendliness. One must be outgoing and meet as many people as possible. It is very important to maintain a positive attitude and to stay focused on doing your best work in all of your assignments. No one enjoys working with a whiner. Most importantly, you must be yourself. People will eventually catch on if you are constantly performing. Smart singers avoid getting sucked into company gossip and avoid personal battles with the other singers. I tell my students when they go to a job that everyone there, when later asked about you, should say that they would love to work with you again. This is true even if (especially if) you didn't enjoy working with that person. If you need to vent about someone (and we all need to do this at times), call a friend or family member at home. This business is far too small to burn any bridges or to treat anyone in a way in which you would not want to be treated yourself.

Finally, the apprentice must take every opportunity offered during the program. If a coach, conductor, or director wants to spend extra time working with you, you must be ready to do so. When you are invited to sing in a master class, you should be the first to volunteer, not the singer hiding in the back because of insecurity or the previous night's festivities. Often singers worry that they're too vocally tired or their arias aren't "ready," and they turn down chances to work with seasoned professionals. This reticence can be fatal. Apprenticeships should serve a dual purpose for you: you should learn as much as you can about your craft, and you should be visible enough that the program becomes a stepping stone to the next level. Many young singers lack the confidence or the knowledge of the business to know how important it is to maximize each apprenticeship. All too many singers are lost on the way up the pyramid structure simply because they don't realize what they need to do.

Double Casting and Covering

Many companies have systems of double casting or covering (understudies), and both of these situations present specific ego-related issues for the singer. Normally singers have their first experiences with double casting at the college or graduate level. Many singers are understandably apprehensive about being constantly compared with their counterparts, and this often leads to defensive behavior. The situation is competitive by definition, after all. Good artists, however, focus on the positive aspects of double casting and minimize the competition.

Singers can learn a great deal from watching and listening to each other if they can move beyond comparison and ranking. As a very young singer, I often found myself cast with singers who were older and more experienced than I was. Several of them were so kind and supportive toward me, letting me apprentice myself to them, that I always tried to return the favor when I happened to be the more seasoned singer. Whether I thought I was "better" than the other singer, I learned that my skills and personality were always different and that my interpretation of the role would inherently have its own flavor. I also got a visual image from which to work while I was sitting out in the house watching the staging.

Inevitably there were days I felt less than on top of my game, and on those days I was grateful to be able to lean on my singing partner. The mutual benefit of such support can be an enormous boon to young singers managing difficult roles for the first time. Nothing makes a rehearsal period seem longer than being in a combative relationship with your double. Some people, of course, refuse to work in a positive way. All you can do in those situations is treat the other singer with courtesy and warmth throughout the process and wait for the ice to break.

While I was on tour with the National Opera Company, I shared my roles with another soprano, and we served as each other's dresser on our off nights. Very early in our tour of Mozart's *Così fan tutte*, my counterpart failed to materialize for Despina's Act I quick change into the Doctor. I tried to give her the benefit of the doubt, thinking that perhaps she had simply missed it accidentally (many thanks, incidentally, to the people backstage who did help me that night). When the same thing happened for the Act II quick change into the Lawyer, I knew I had a problem.

The next day we traveled to another city, and I spent a large portion of the trip thinking about the best way to handle the situation. I knew the other soprano was expecting me to be absent for her quick changes at that evening's performance in retaliation. But this was October in a September through May contract, and I didn't want to continue in this vein. I needed her help and support for the rest of the tour. Finally I decided to be as professional as possible and complete her changes, "kill them with kindness" as the saying goes. I went further than necessary, hanging up her costumes for her and even asking if I could get her some water. By the end of the evening, she was so embarrassed she could barely meet my eyes. She never missed my costume changes again.

The relationship between the cover (understudy) and the singer is less equal by definition, which can either be easier or more difficult. When the two singers are very close in professional level, or they are both students, this relationship is usually fairly tense. I have been in at least one situation in which the singer covering me was another student, and it was unpleasant from start to finish. She refused ever to sing the role at any rehearsal, made a great show of doing other things (knitting, reading) while I was singing, and ridiculed my costume at the dress rehearsal. I suppose her tactics achieved the desired effect. One of the reasons I didn't audition for the next opera at the university was that I knew I would most likely be double cast with her, and the role itself was not attractive enough to me to make it worth dealing with her again.

Most cover situations occur with professional companies, and it is critical to be both respectful of the artist you're covering and ready to jump in at any time. Every time I have covered a role professionally, I have ended up onstage eventually, whether it was a performance or a rehearsal. Singers must learn to treat these roles as though they have been hired to perform them because, in effect, they have. With very prestigious companies, a distinction is sometimes made between performance covers and rehearsal covers. Singers should always clarify whether they would go on in the absence of the original artist. This can sometimes make the difference in whether a young singer should accept a contract to cover a particularly heavy role.

Covering a role is more difficult than actually singing it in one important way: if you find yourself onstage, you will not have had the rehearsal time, either musically or dramatically, that the principal artist has had. What you will have had is a lot of time sitting and observing. You must walk through all staging every night at home and take advantage of any musical coaching you can get with the conductor, just in case. If you do go on, your voice will be fresh, and the cast will be on your side because everyone loves an underdog. The annals are full of careers made when singers stepped in for ailing stars. Critics focus on the luck involved in these events, but it is always truly solid preparation that allows these singers to make the most of these opportunities.

During my first professional job at the Ash Lawn-Highland Festival, I learned about the ups and downs of covering. I was hired to sing Papagena and the Second Lady in *The Magic Flute*, to be a performance cover for Pamina, and, to flesh out my contract, a rehearsal cover for both Serpina in *La serva padrona* by Pergolesi and Lucy in *The Telephone* by Menotti. I was in essence the extra woman needed to cover all of the roles in *The Magic Flute* in case of illness on any given night. The season also included *Daughter of the Regiment* by Donizetti, but I was not cast as Marie, largely because I had not sung any high notes at my audition, although I did get the chance to tour in the role later on with the National Opera Company. (See Chapter Four.)

Eventually, the soprano I was covering became ill, and I sang three performances as Pamina. During the intermission of my last performance, Denise* came backstage into the women's dressing room to announce that she would be coming back for the next show. Getting no reaction from me, she called out, "Oh, Lynn, about your ex-boyfriend." I had recently ended a three-year relationship in a very public way, and the topic was strictly off-limits.

I told her I had no interest in anything she might have to say about him, and she smiled and said, "Oh, it's just that I have a friend who's dating him now."

I felt as though I'd been punched in the stomach. Fortunately, Ash Lawn held forty-five minute intermissions to allow for audience picnics on the grounds, former President James Monroe's plantation. I had a lot of time to think about why someone would go out of her way to upset me and then to get angry. I thought about what my father used to say: "Don't get mad, get even."

I went out for Act II and sang better than I ever had before. I put my very heart and soul into the aria "Ach, ich fühl's." I knew that Denise simply thought I would crumble if she pushed me hard enough, and she obviously thought my singing was good enough to want me to falter. The best thing I could do to regain my footing was to sing as well as possible and refuse to be intimidated. I was still young enough to be surprised that someone would deliberately hurt me, but I had enough time to work through it. I knew I had done well when Denise left just after I sang the aria.

I learned another important lesson that summer when the director of the one-act operas asked me and the bass in the program to come the following day to walk through the Pergolesi and the Menotti operas for her. I had learned the music very well, but I wasn't completely memorized, and I certainly didn't have all of the staging in my head. Both Serpina and Lucy were triple cast, in addition to me, and the conductor had assured me that I was not a performance cover. I was also consumed by juggling three different roles in the Mozart, the largest of which I never really got to rehearse. Still, it was humiliating to stumble through the other roles and to be lectured by the director, rightly so, for neglecting my responsibility. I also knew I had squandered the chance to make a positive connection with her.

During my years as a member of the Opera Company of Philadelphia Chorus, I witnessed several fine examples of professional covering. One afternoon about a week before the opening of Menotti's *The Saint of Bleecker Street*, with Menotti himself directing, the mezzo-soprano singing the pivotal role of Desideria had still not arrived. Menotti was livid, but the production staff decided to allow the student rehearsal cover, Jody Kidwell, to sing the run-through. She made the most of her opportunity and gave a fabulous performance. When the original artist appeared, she was not nearly as well prepared, and she eventually withdrew from the production. Jody was awarded the role, even though she was not technically a performance cover. Practically every singer in Philadelphia was in the enormous chorus, and we were all thrilled for "our" girl.

James Caputo was another strong example when he covered Franco Farina as Pinkerton in Puccini's *Madame Butterfly*. Farina was fairly late on the scene, so Jim sang many of the rehearsals alongside Diana Soviero as Butterfly. Jim was in his early twenties at the time, but he handled it all with extreme confidence. Most impressive was the Italian he threw back and forth with the conductor Eduardo Mueller at the orchestra rehearsal. Jim's fluency and aplomb in front of this major ensemble inspired me to take a language immersion program in Italian the following summer.

Financial Drain

Beginning a career as a professional singer is an expensive proposition, and the sheer cost involved stops many people along the way. Apprenticeships and covers, even if you are fortunate enough to get them, don't pay particularly well. Voice lessons are a necessity, and most singers supplement these with coachings. Audition fees are always rising, not to mention the cost of hiring your own pianist whenever it's an especially important audition or you're listing a notoriously difficult piece.

When I moved to New York, I took a voice lesson every third week (at the now low price of $100 an hour—$150 is standard for an hour-long lesson today) and coachings with two other pianists on the other weeks (at $40 each, also a bargain by today's standards). I could only do this because I had already been with my voice teacher for three years. Glenn Morton knew my best sound and told me when I had it. Glenn was also an angel on earth, one of the kindest people I knew, which helped a lot in New York. My other coach, Kevin Jones, had fantastic ears and picked up on every detail. When I wanted something to be perfect (which was all the time), I went to see Kevin. The fact that I'm also a pianist saved me additional coaching costs because some singers have to pay pianists to teach them the notes, the languages, and all kinds of other details. It all adds up very quickly.

Most serious classical singers eventually decide to move to New York City, the home of most of the auditions, teachers, coaches, agents, and other forms of serious career networking. New York is an exorbitantly expensive place to live, of course, even without the extra cost of vocal training. When I first arrived, I planned to support myself by accompanying voice lessons. I learned quite a bit

about voice teaching during the months that I did this, but I found
the work ultimately to be too sporadic. It began to feel like I was
trying to launch two shaky careers instead of just one.

Like most singers in New York, I turned to temporary work.
None of us wanted to wait tables because of the wear and tear on our
voices, and most of us were organized and presented well enough to
make competent office workers. At first I worked as a receptionist,
but I couldn't live in Manhattan on eight dollars an hour, so I
borrowed money from the Bank of Mom and Dad to take a
computer class. I then found a steady temp job at American Express
Travel, where I stayed for two years, eventually making eighteen
dollars an hour. The people there were great, always finding me new
assignments within the group and allowing me to leave whenever I
needed to for auditions and lessons. They eventually offered me a
management job as a trainer in Learning and Development just
before I left New York, but my heart was not in a career in business.

Although I was lucky enough to find a reasonable situation,
temping can become degrading at times for many singers. Most of us
have graduate degrees, and we are quite obviously overqualified for
our positions. (See the wickedly funny novel *The Devil Wears Prada*
by Lauren Weisberger.) The key to maintaining personal dignity
seems to lie in how we are treated by management. It is a tricky social
arrangement, being one of the secretaries but also being a professional of sorts. The singers who come from family money and don't
have to do any of this have an enormous advantage, one they don't
always appreciate. Many singers simply run out of resources to keep
trying to run a singing career, and they either accept permanent jobs
with corporations, or leave New York entirely in search of a new life.

One of the most disturbing phenomena in New York (and now,
other major cities as well) is the cottage industry that has sprung up
to make (or should it be take?) money from all of the people who
want to be opera singers. The teacher in me says that everyone
deserves the chance to try, but I don't feel it is right for people to ex-
ploit the dreams of others for their own financial gain. Many of these
singers have no real career prospects at all, but they have been

convinced by someone that if they just take the right workshop, or work with the right teacher, this time everything will come together. Soprano Renee Fleming even commissioned a song about it in 1996, "Another New Voice Teacher" by Andrew Thomas with lyrics by Gene Scheer.

By the time I left New York, I had seen too many singers in their late thirties and forties having slogged it out for years and years to no avail, still waiting for that magic voice teacher to come along. (I'm not speaking here about singers who turn to classical voice later in their careers.) It was always sobering to meet these singers and to wonder if my perceptions of my own talent were any less skewed than theirs seemed to be. At any rate, when my students prepare to pay for any level of training, we consider the actual benefits very carefully.

Reviews

My teacher used to say that if you believed the good reviews, you had to believe the bad ones as well, so you were better off not reading them at all. Most of us don't have that much self-control. The fact is, each review represents one person's opinion, and it must be taken it as such no matter how influential the reviewer may seem to be.

I once received three different reviews on the same night for my performance as Lauretta in *Gianni Schicchi* by Puccini with the National Opera Company in Raleigh, North Carolina. The first read, "Praise should go to lovely soprano Lynn Eustis singing in crystalline English," and the second said that both the tenor and I "sang beautifully with tender tone." The third review started off well: "As Lauretta, Lynn Eustis looked lovely, a Botticellian figure with *pianissimos* as pure as if she'd plucked them right out of the ether." Great, right? But the review went on: "But she sang her aria so lethargically that it might as well have been a plea to get thee to a nunnery." When these reviews appeared, our conductor sputtered, "I almost had to repeat the aria because of the audience response." I learned from that experience that validation didn't come from what it said in the paper about my performance. I had already received my thanks from the audience and the conductor.

Sometimes reviews do have an effect on employment, particularly the good ones. If a conductor really believes in your work, he will not be influenced by poor reviews. Chances are good that he himself has been panned by the same reviewer. Good reviews, however, do tend to lead to increased professional attention, particularly if they come from multiple sources. If you travel frequently to sing, you are often long gone by the time the review appears, and the impact may feel less severe.

I am very frank with my students about the reviews I receive, especially the ones in the Dallas Morning News, partially because I know they will see them. I also see them as teaching opportunities. At the present time there are two classical music reviewers for the Dallas paper: one seems to generally enjoy my singing and another is for some reason not touched by my work. I know when I read the byline what the review will say about me, regardless of what I thought about my own performance, and that has been painful at times. I talk with my students about it because I want them to know that my true "review" of the performance is based on my own opinion and that of the conductor. If the reviewer liked what I did, this is "gravy."

Last spring, I received a call from a disgruntled Dallas Bach Society subscriber. This gentleman was upset about my latest lukewarm review in the paper. He told me that he and his wife loved my voice and felt that I got "better and better" every time they heard me. I cannot express how gratifying it was to me that this man would call me at the university to share this with me. (He said he had also called the Dallas Bach Society conductor.) After that call, I knew I had reached at least two people and not just on that one occasion, which is, after all, my reason for singing in the first place.

Further Exploration

1. How many opera auditions have you done (roughly)? _____
   Has it become easier as you have done more of them? _____
   If not, what is the most difficult aspect of them for you?

   _____

   _____

2. If you have done an apprenticeship, which group do you think you
   belonged to?_____ stars___ middle ground____struggling group

   Were you asked to do any extra coaching or rehearsing (including
   master class performances)? If so, did you take advantage of the
   opportunity?

   _____

   _____

   What did you learn about the way "the business" works from your
   time there?_____

   _____

   Were you invited back for a second summer? _____ If not,
   why not?

   _____

   _____

3. Considering your "best" and "worst" double casting experiences, is
   there anything you would do differently today in either situation?

   _____

   _____

4. List any roles you have covered:

Role	Opera	Artist you covered
_____	_____	_____
_____	_____	_____
_____	_____	_____
_____	_____	_____

Did you ever go onstage in either rehearsals or in performances?

_____

_____

Was the artist gracious to you? Were you gracious to him or her?

_____

_____

_____

If you have been in a production in which a cover went on, describe the experience._____

_____

_____

5. What are you currently paying (or charging) per hour for:
Voice lessons: _____ Coachings: _____

Are you prepared to make major financial sacrifices to have a career as a singer? What other job skills do you have that you will be able to use in the meantime?

_____

_____

6. What is your gut reaction when you are reviewed (in print):
Positively_____
Neutrally_____
Negatively_____

In each case, how closely did the reviewer match what you thought about your own performance? What the conductor thought? How the audience responded?

_____

_____

_____

_____

_____

Were you able to move on to your next project effectively? _____

_____

_____

Chapter Nine: Teaching—It's Not for Everyone

What Teaching Is and Isn't

Growing up in a family of educators, I have always hated the saying, "Those who can't do, teach." In most fields, one must be able to "do" as an essential condition for being able to teach. Teaching is a completely different skill with its own set of requisite abilities in addition to the demands of the field. An effective teacher not only imparts information in a clear manner but motivates students to want to learn the material and think for themselves. These skills are unrelated to performance ability in any field; music is no exception.

The misconception that being proficient as a performer automatically qualifies one as a competent teacher is perhaps even more common in voice because of the internal, unseen nature of the instrument. Just as some instrumental teachers can't see the hand position or fingering needed to make a warmer sound or tune the note more accurately, some wonderfully gifted singers are completely ineffective as teachers. Some natural singers never figure out what it is they're doing, or how their own sensations are different from what other singers feel. The larger the voice, the more this seems to hold true when the singer becomes a teacher.

Many natural singers also have trouble empathizing with young singers who experience performance anxiety. Singers whose voices have never failed them don't have any understanding of what it means to be afraid to sing in a public situation. I have had conversations with confident artists turned teachers who were horrified because a student cried during a lesson. I have difficulty reassuring these lucky beings that such behavior is normal for young female singers. In a similar vein, singers who have had easy professional careers along with early and continuous success also tend to lack empathy. They are not insensitive people; they merely have no context in which to put the average singer's struggle.

On the other hand, it is difficult to name outstanding teachers who do not sing well. Good teachers do not need an abundance of vocal talent, but they do need to use their instruments efficiently and artistically. Teaching is not a good place for singers who have had vocal problems and have not reached a full understanding of why these problems occurred. Some singers approach it as a second career when the first career doesn't pan out. If these singers have worked out their vocal issues, however, they can become the most empathetic teachers of all, with the deepest, most personal knowledge of vocal technique.

Teaching is not a fallback career, contrary to popular opinion. When singers say, "I can always teach if I don't make it as a performer," I cringe. Teaching is not for you if you would rather be a full-time performer, are a failed performer, or have unresolved ambitions of your own. It will be too difficult, understandable though it is, to put the students first and manage residual bitterness. We have to be in a place emotionally where we can be genuinely happy for our students' successes, especially if they should surpass our own performance careers at any point. The teaching profession has many outstanding members who care about the students but more are always welcome. One of the reasons I wanted to become a voice teacher was that I looked around and saw too many people teaching by default. I wanted to see more people teaching as a first choice, and I hoped that by choosing it first myself, I might inspire other smart, empathetic singers to choose teaching.

I recently told an artist friend beginning a teaching career that you simply need two things to teach studio voice well:

1) You have to have good ears.
2) You have to care about people.

Having good ears means a great variety of things. To begin with, you must be analytical about what you hear, you must have a detailed understanding of musical styles, you must be able to think in both the long and short terms for your student's growth, and you must have an ear for languages and intonation.

When students put their voices into your hands, they trust your aesthetic as much as anything else about you. They know you will make dozens of tiny decisions at every lesson that will influence the tonal course their voices will take, as the eye doctor repeatedly asks you, "Better one, or better two?" to determine your prescription. All voice teachers teach technique according to their aesthetic preferences. Occasionally, I have had differences of opinion about technique with a colleague, only to realize that what we disagree about is actually aesthetic in nature. We are not at odds technically when I know that my technique will not produce the sound the other teacher has in mind, and the reverse is equally true.

Caring about people is just as vital to effective voice teaching as having good ears. Voice teachers deal with students as individuals and they must consider each person as a human being first. The best teacher-student relationships are based on mutual trust. Trust only happens when two people know and accept each other without personal judgment. Every student comes with a unique set of experiences, both in singing and in "real life," and the teacher must relate slightly differently to each one. The students can tell immediately if the teacher is not interested in knowing them as people and only in offering identical technical information to all. When the teacher considers "the voice" the sum total of the student's interest as a person, he cannot develop authentic confidence in the student. Pablo Picasso put it bluntly in a 1957 article for *The New Yorker*:

> How could it be possible to feel no interest in other people and, because of an ivory-tower indifference, detach yourself from the life they bring with such open full hands?[1]

A large component of humane teaching is knowing how much to say and when to say it. The better I know the student, the more accurately I can assess what he or she is ready to hear. I can also determine what I will need to say to lead him or her further down the path. The students will go much further emotionally, musically, and technically than they expect to if they believe that you think they are capable. If you are sitting back in judgment, trying to apply "reverse psychology" to tempt them into showing you something, it will backfire more often than not. Like any manipulative technique, it is best applied sparingly.

Studio voice is, of course, only one form of teaching, and a highly specialized one. The field of music education is ultimately much more widely influential, and I consider the work of music education students to be critically important. These are the people who are going to teach children from the time they are small until they graduate from high school, long before most studio voice teachers ever encounter them. They will instill a love of music in these students, we hope, and lay the foundation for all of their future learning in music. When I finished my own student teaching (middle and high school) in Pennsylvania, I left with a certain amount of guilt and the nagging feeling that I had left something undone, something vital that must be done by our best musicians and highest quality human beings.

Ultimately, being a good teacher is about being your authentic self with the students, which doesn't come naturally to everyone. The more open you are willing to be about who you are, the more open your students will be about who they are, which leads to a free sense of confidence and deeper truth in artistry. In his thoughtful book *The Courage to Teach* Parker J. Palmer notes, "Good teaching cannot be reduced to technique; good teaching comes from the identity and integrity of the teacher...good teachers join self and subject and students in the fabric of life."[2] If you have the courage to stay close to the students, without distancing yourself to feel secure, you have the beginnings of a satisfying teaching life.

Considering Other Options in Music

For open-minded singers, career interests can develop and flow naturally. Some singers go directly into lives as professional opera singers. Others combine a variety of musical pursuits into their lives. In my position at the University of North Texas, I am very fortunate because I have a good deal of autonomy over my activities. I teach studio voice, serve as chair of the Graduate Performance Committee (overseeing policies and procedures for our 500+ DMA and MM performance students), sing professionally off-campus, give frequent recitals on-campus, and spend considerable time writing (as this book evidences). I also adjudicate at various student competitions, and I present a lecture/recital on music of the Holocaust from time to time around the country. I relish the freedom I have to follow so many different loves of mine. I am much happier juggling all of these projects (of my own choosing) than I ever was pursuing an operatic career.

As a teacher, I try to steer singers toward the fields in which I think they will be both most successful and happiest on a personal level. Some of them will be suited to a traditional operatic career, but the majority will form hybrid careers of their own. The more I know about the options, and the more I know about my students' personalities and interests, the better I can help them create fulfilling musical lives. Not all of them have the complete package for opera or the intellectual interest in an academic career. While I received outstanding training during all three of my degrees, I think that all music programs could do more to educate students about career options. The thinking seems to be that all performance majors should shoot for the Metropolitan Opera, but that is an unrealistic goal for just about all of them. These singers do not have to throw out the baby with the bath water just because they won't become international opera stars. Even if they are going to succeed in that field, there are more possible roads to take to get there every year.

For example, many light-voiced, intelligent singers have begun coming up through the early music ranks, specializing in Baroque opera at first and then moving into Mozart and other Classical era works. Some sopranos who have done this recently include Dorothea Röschmann, Sandrine Piau, Patricia Petibon, Sophie Daneman, Christine Brandes, and Lisa Saffer. If young singers approach early music from a proper technical standpoint, they will not injure or otherwise "hold back" their voices. Early music has much to teach singers in the areas of communication, style, articulation, intonation, and ensemble. My singers who participate in our Collegium Musicum under Lyle Nordstrom find that their work there informs all of their other solo work. Several of them have already begun to find work in the summers through early music programs.

The singers who possess the analytical skills necessary for early music are often encouraged to pursue graduate degrees in musicology. These degrees further their knowledge of performance practices and vastly increase the singer's credibility within the academic community. Working on a combination of early music performance and musicology can lead to an academic position as a voice or musicology professor or a career as an early music or oratorio soloist. The same clarity of pitch and intellectual ability required for early music often lands singers in contemporary music as well. One of the most rampant stereotypes about the music world, in fact, is that the smartest, most esoteric and eccentric people can be found at either end of the spectrum, in early music and in contemporary music.

If the student is a talented writer and wants to avoid performance and academia, a career as a classical music critic is a possible choice. (No one would argue against the notion that the business can always use an intelligent, empathetic music critic!) Singers with these skills often read music well enough to supplement any of the above with work as a professional chorister. Most major cities now have a symphony chorus, an opera chorus, and at least one or two independent professional choirs.

Musical theater is arguably an even tougher business than opera in which to succeed based on the sheer numbers of people involved, but it is nevertheless the appropriate field for some talented voice students. The singer must have enough of a "look" to survive the typing auditions, in which ten or more singers are lined up in a room with their head shots while the directors of the show then decide which singers will have the chance to stay and sing. The singer must also be able to act at least as well as he sings, and, if possible, dance. (My comic friend, Jim David, used to refer to a particular artist as a "triple threat: can't act, can't sing, can't dance.") I generally allow my younger students to sing legitimate musical theater pieces for me in addition to their classical repertoire, partly because I would rather they do this with my supervision than without it. Some of these students will simply have a better chance at a career in this repertoire.

For the singers who have good leadership abilities, I may suggest directing or conducting. Directors have strong sense of the visual and emotional, and they also need a good rapport with the singers. I have a wonderful singer/actress right now who sees what the singers need to be doing and knows how to communicate it to them in a way that makes them believe they can do it. If the singer has exceptional keyboard skills and understands the balance between the details and the big picture musically, a career as a conductor or as an opera coach can be an option. The singer who is organized, presents well, and can handle not being directly involved in the art form itself is an excellent candidate for a graduate degree in arts administration. At this writing there are many fine programs across the country, and there is a great need for knowledgeable people who truly care about the arts to keep funding alive through responsible management.

Some of the newest programs in music include music therapy and music and medicine. Music therapy explores the healing powers of music with a variety of illnesses, both physical and behavioral. The rapidly growing field of music and medicine focused on performance anxiety and performance-related injuries is in its initial stages, but it has grown to cover a wide variety of physical and emotional issues for musicians. As the area of sports psychology has grown, these disciplines have begun sharing information.

None of these alternate careers is viable, however, for a singer who would still truly rather sing opera. We talk about options simply to let singers know that they exist and take the conversation from there. Most teachers admit to having used the phrase, "Have you ever thought about a career in ...?" If we handle these situations with careful thought and compassion, we can make real differences in our students' lives. As I have already said, each singer must find his or her own path. For some people, it is less painful to leave the music profession altogether than it is to compromise on the area of involvement.

Leaving Music Entirely

While I was a student at Curtis, one of the other students was dismissed from the opera program. This singer had always had a special aptitude for languages, and he told us that he was planning to become a translator for the United Nations. Robert* held a big sale (Everything Must Go!) at his apartment to liquidate his substantial collection of scores and CDs at bargain prices. I picked up a few great deals myself. He had a ceremonial hurling-out-of-the-window of his humidifier, which he called a "germ factory." All things considered, he took the whole thing very well.

They say that if you can be happy doing something else, you should go do it, and Robert clearly fit that category. It's not always that simple. For many people, leaving music is a difficult decision, one that doesn't always stick. It's the kind of decision you can only reach for yourself. No one else can tell you when it's time. Some people are much happier once they stop trying to follow the dream and relegate it to a hobby. It becomes something fun again instead of something that controls every second of your life, something that makes you constantly feel inadequate or guilty.

Several of my students improved dramatically as singers as soon as they dropped the performance components of their degrees. In every case, they were surprised by how much freer and more enjoyable it had become, but I wasn't. My own singing seemed to come flowing out of my body after I left New York and took some of the pressure off myself. I had decided to go back to school and focus on my doctoral degree, but, oddly enough, the singing jobs started pouring in. I was able to find a new love for my voice and for my singing, and I found myself singing more often than I ever had while I was living in New York. I felt differently about it, though; it didn't define me anymore. I've known many people with similar feelings.

I know now that I was one of the lucky ones. Of the twenty-seven singers who attended Curtis with me over three years, three have sung at the Metropolitan Opera, seven others continue to have healthy operatic careers, at least four have given up singing entirely, and I have no idea what happened to any of the others. The odds are not in our favor when we embark upon a singing career. If we love to sing, we go as far as we can go before our voices or our temperaments take us down another path. When I left New York, I expected many of my Curtis friends to chastise me. Instead, the most common response was, "I wish I had something else I really wanted to do."

Although there are many ways to have a career in music, not everyone is meant to stay in the field on the professional level. Music has great restorative powers for everyone, whether or not you're drawing a paycheck from your involvement. During my summers at the Belvoir Terrace program in Lenox, Massachusetts, I learned from Nancy Goldberg that the important concept to teach the girls was respect for and enjoyment of the arts. They weren't all going to be musicians, but the arts need patrons, patrons who understand what is involved in the process. The same is true for students of music on any level. Music enriches our lives, and time spent learning about it and doing it is never wasted time, whatever the professional outcome. As Christopher Morley said in *Where the Blue Begins*, "There is only one success—to be able to spend your life in your own way."[3]

Notes

1. George Seldes, compiler, *The Great Quotations* (New York: Lyle Stuart, 1960), 562.
2. Parker J. Palmer, *The Courage to Teach* (San Francisco: Jossey-Bass, 1998), 10–11.
3. Seldes, 507.

Appendix A:
Working with Beginning Singers

Being a student's first voice teacher is an enormous responsibility. You will set the emotional tone for the student's vocal life from this day forward: how they will see their voice in relation to themselves, themselves in relation to the teacher, their teacher in relation to their technique, and their technique in relation to their artistry. Each of these interactions is critical to the singer's success. If singers learn unhealthy habits at the beginning, they will spend years undoing the damage, if that's even possible.

Many new studio voice teachers are blissfully unaware of these implications, as I was when I began teaching. On that first day, we think we are just warming up the singer, making some comments, and assigning repertoire. We have no idea that what we say will resonate in the student's mind and heart for years to come. The most offhanded remarks we make about their voices live on to shape their vocal egos until they study with another teacher, and sometimes our remarks survive even then. These students are fragile when they come to us. Maybe they have never sung alone in front of anyone before, and their ownership of their voice is still very personal and private. To some degree, it will always remain this way, but this first exposure before "someone who knows" is significant.

For many young singers, the most difficult part of beginning study is becoming accustomed to singing alone for someone else's critique. As voice teachers, we take this for granted because we are used to it, but many beginning students have not spent significant amounts of time singing alone in front of others. This can be true even at the college level; many freshmen, in fact, have spent the majority of their vocal time in ensembles, taking the occasional solo or being part of a quartet but not performing alone on any consistent basis. It takes many singers a long time simply to become comfortable making a full sound, using all of their breath, and being confident enough not to hide behind others. It is important for teachers to demonstrate often at the beginning, to help give them assurance and to let them find their voices, not overloading them with too much technical information all at once. When I work with very young singers (twelve and younger), they are often shocked at first when I demonstrate an exercise. They look at me in horror and say, "I can't do THAT!" I usually point out that I've been doing it a lot longer than they have, and everyone's voice is different: I can't wait to hear what their voice sounds like!

Recently, I lent one of my graduate students a copy of Willa Cather's *Song of the Lark*. This novel should be required reading for any aspiring singer. Cather intended it as an allegory of her own writing career, but somehow she captured exactly the artistic yearnings of young singers and what it means to carry your talent within you. My student and friend Lynne was especially touched by this passage, as I was when I first read the book:

> She knew, of course, that there was something about her that was different. But it was more like a friendly spirit than like anything that was a part of herself. She brought everything to it, and it answered her; happiness consisted of that backward and forward movement of herself. The something came and went, she never knew how. Sometimes she hunted for it and could not find it; again, she lifted her eyes from a book, or stepped out-of-doors, or wakened in the morning, and it was there—under her cheek, it usually seemed to be, or over her breast—a kind of warm sureness. And when it was there, everything was more interesting and beautiful, even people.

As teachers of young singers we must acknowledge our role as protectors of the special thing within each of our students. We must take care not to do anything to jeopardize the safety of that profound, sacred thing. Our students present it to us so trustingly, and we cannot be reckless with such a meaningful gift.

The First Lesson—Making the Agreement

When potential students call me to "take a lesson," I always re-title the session a "consultation." I tell the singer to come warmed-up if possible, prepared to sing two contrasting pieces. After they sing these pieces for me, I will offer my thoughts on what they are doing well, what I think can be improved, and whether I think I can help them. If I cannot offer them a place in my studio, I always offer other options for them to pursue. If I think I may be able to take the student, I move into some technical exercises based on the issues I heard, to determine how well we would work together.

If we are to avoid inflicting damage (the physician's creed, "first do no harm," comes to mind) we must focus first on the positive aspects of what the students bring to us. Whenever I hear a new student, I say something positive immediately upon the conclusion of the first piece. There is always something good to be said, even if it's as general as "I loved your enjoyment of the piece." The singer has just exposed him or herself to you, and this is a vulnerable moment. The encouragement you offer or don't offer at this point will be indicative of your future relationship.

The tone of the next portion of the conversation, the diagnosis, is even more crucial to gauge correctly for each person. In my experience, too many teachers look for safety in the extremes. They may minimize the negative aspects of the diagnosis to the point where they don't actually relay them to the student in an attempt to avoid the student's possible emotional reaction. At the opposite extreme, the teacher assumes an authoritative posture and begins to dictate a laundry list of faults, making any sort of recovery seem out of the question. In the first scenario, the student is given a false sense of security, one that ultimately proves frustrating when the student knows that something is wrong but is told that everything is fine. In the second, the student walks away shattered, utterly dependent on the teacher to rebuild his or her self-image, which was perhaps the teacher's design in setting up such a situation.

I find it much easier to tell students the simple truth about what I hear in a calm, practical, and supportive way. Chances are good that they already know what their biggest problems are; I often begin this discussion by asking them what they think just to make sure. My honesty is usually appreciated. If the student is not interested in hearing the truth, he or she is probably not truly ready to begin serious vocal study. It is most important to offer immediate analysis that assures the student of your belief in the possibility of success. The student wants to know what the problems are, whether or not you think they can be fixed, and whether or not you are willing to help fix them. I don't promise perfect results, but I do guarantee that we can make changes if the student is willing work at least as hard as I do. The more excited I get about the potential for the student's voice, the more inspired the student becomes to start working. I believe that setting up this agreement between teacher and student is absolutely necessary for any meaningful improvement, and it should happen at the first meeting.

Once you decide to move into the exercises, you must effect positive change in the student's sound before the student leaves. You may have covered a wide variety of issues during your conversation about where things will go, but now you must give the student something concrete to practice until the next lesson. If you can make an audible change, one that also feels easier for the student, you will further inspire the student to go with you down a new technical pathway. This should not be a band-aid, or something temporary, but a step in a new direction. When the student experiences a small measure of success with the new ideas, he or she will be eager to keep the work going upon leaving the studio that day. Your shared success cements the agreement you have created, the new team you have formed to build the student's new life as a singer.

Moving Slowly—Technique and Repertoire

In working with beginning singers, the teacher must be mindful of which technical aspects should be addressed first and which aspects should come later in the student's development. Many volumes have already been written advising voice teachers on where to start, and there are almost as many opinions on the subject as there are voice teachers. My view is that many young singers, particularly at the high school and undergraduate levels, are pushed into advanced repertoire before they have mastered the basic elements of technique. Many of the reasons for this haste have been explored earlier in this book. The effects on the singer's confidence, however, are not easy to quantify when the flashy piece she could manage at age fifteen is no longer possible for her at age twenty.

The basic elements of technique, for me, are the coordinated onset and release (based in the use of the breath), matching of vowel sounds, and basic *sostenuto* (line) between notes. Without these building blocks, the student will be unable to sing even the simplest pieces in a technically healthy manner. Repetition is key, and the student must practice using these elements correctly in a variety of pieces before attempting more difficult techniques. I often use the Panofka, Op. 85, vocalises[2] on different vowels, and the Vaccai exercises[3] in Italian to create touchstones the students can return to later, should their voices begin to lose flexibility. I personally find it helpful to have a set of exercises that my muscles remember correctly, to which I can turn whenever my voice just doesn't feel right.

During the beginning stages, there must be no rush to move into more operatic techniques, such as *aggiustamento*, extremes of range, heavy weight in the middle voice, highly developed chest voice, and extended *coloratura* passages. For some singers, these elements will not truly come into the voice until they begin graduate study. Whenever the student begins to lose control of the aforementioned basic techniques, he or she should step away from the more advanced repertoire and return to the basic exercises until the voice is functioning properly again. Many teachers are reluctant to spend enough time solidifying the basic technique or to return to it when problems develop. Moving students into professional-level repertoire too quickly can cause irreparable damage to their psyches as well as to their instruments. When they begin this repertoire in high school, they often have a difficult time emotionally when their college voice teacher moves them "backward" into more basic material. They will always face crises of confidence when their technique begins to fail as a result of excessive demands on the instrument, just as athletes do when their physical abilities fail them.

Another checkpoint for the appropriateness of the repertoire is whether the student is able to communicate its emotional and dramatic content without losing technical control. When the emotions of the piece are too complex for a young singer to handle, the piece is usually too difficult from a technical standpoint as well. The teacher must choose pieces straightforward enough to allow the student to keep all of the "balls in the air" (musical, technical, dramatic), to use a juggling metaphor. The difficulty level should rise only when the student can handle the next level reasonably well in all of these areas. Of course, many pieces have multiple levels at which the student will understand them over the course of his or her musical life.

Ultimately it will be much easier for a healthy singer to advance quickly later in the career than it will be for an unhealthy singer to undo vocal and emotional damage, which is perhaps the most persuasive argument for moving slowly with both technique and repertoire.

Beginning Lessons—For the Singer

The studio voice experience is mysterious and wide-ranging, and most new voice students have no clear idea what to expect. Because they have no standard against which to compare it, they tend to accept whatever happens in this first student/teacher arrangement as the norm. The student is vulnerable by definition; there are few ways for him or her to judge, for example, whether the technical information is correct. We take a necessary leap of faith when we attempt to do what our teacher asks of us. Even when we know the information goes against something that we believe is true or that we have learned from a previous teacher, we can easily be convinced to change our perspective. "You wouldn't be taking voice lessons if you always wanted to sound exactly the way you do now, would you?"

one teacher reasonably asked me when I questioned a seemingly controversial technical concept.

As frightening as this relative lack of knowledge can be, there are some ways for new students to assess their situation. First and foremost, the student must feel a sense of personal compatibility with the teacher. If the teacher seems cold or out of reach, he or she will probably remain that way. If you need someone warmer and more open, keep looking. I have already noted that people sing as they are, and if they are effective teachers, they teach as they are to an even greater degree. My teaching style is very honest and personal, and not every student is comfortable with that level of exposure. I meet personally with singers before I accept them into my studio because I know that I am not the right teacher for everyone. As a student, you should pay attention to any personal red flags, any signs that you are going to have serious difficulty connecting with this teacher as one human being to another.

The next expectation you must have is a clear analysis of your work, one that is unflinching about your technical strengths and weaknesses. I am constantly surprised by the number of new students who tell me that this is the first time anyone has ever addressed their technical issues so frankly and practically. It has always seemed to me that this is the very definition of the job. If your new teacher does not speak clearly about your problems, you should ask questions about what she will want to change about your singing. You should also ask for specific information on how she plans to approach these changes. If the answers to these questions seem vague, you may want to consult with a few other teachers for comparison.

I also feel it is important for the teacher to have musical ideas and to assess what needs to best draw out the student's musical personality. Because issues of style and temperament are so closely related to technique, the teacher must be able to choose repertoire wisely and guide the student through the music stylistically. Teachers who don't subscribe to this view tend to present a single block of technical information in exactly the same way to each and every student. In most cases, these students all have a similar tone quality, and this tone quality varies little between musical styles.

With regard to my own vocal study, I realize in retrospect that spending five years with a "technique" teacher was too safe for me, and I used this safety net as a way to avoid becoming a more expressive artist. After the vocal problems I had as a student at Curtis, I was reassured to have a teacher who said things like, "It doesn't matter what the temperature was in your hotel room last night, or whether the planets are perfectly aligned. If you do these things physically, these sounds will result." At first this approach helped me to regain my confidence in my vocal endurance. Since I had always been a technically proficient singer naturally, however, it was too easy for me to push the music aside as something I would "do in my coachings." In fairness to my teacher, she tried to animate me during the lessons, and I don't blame her for my shortcomings as a performer. My point is simply that I might have progressed further with a less pragmatic, more emotionally demanding teacher.

Finally, the prospective student should consider the strength of the teacher's own vocal ego. This can be difficult for a young singer to evaluate beyond a simple gut feeling, but there are questions he or she should consider. How does the teacher speak about him or herself? Is she eager to tell you every little thing he or she has done lately, or is he or she humble, even matter-of-fact, about professional life? Does he or she seem to want your approval? Is he or she reluctant to admit mistakes or be open about them? Do you have his or her full attention during the lesson? Perhaps most importantly, how does he or she treat other students and colleagues? If you sense that any aspect of your success will be motivated by a need for gratification, you should think carefully about entering into this relationship. Your teacher should be happy for you but not dependent on your success.

The student/teacher relationship is a very special, demanding, frustrating, emotional, satisfying, joyful place when it is healthy. I have learned a great deal from teachers with whom I did not have this magical personal connection. The most influential people in my life, teachers official or otherwise, have all taken the time to know me as a person, to see beyond my voice, and to offer themselves as real human beings with flaws and quirks of their own. Through knowing them, I learned that my own idiosyncrasies were what made me special, and that my voice was simply one aspect of me as a person and what I had to offer the world around me. I have been blessed to know these wonderful people, and I am blessed all over again by the next generation of fantastic individuals I now know as my students.

Notes

1. Willa Cather, *Song of the Lark* (New York: Penguin Books, 1991), 70.
2. Heinrich Panofka, *Twenty-Four Progressive Vocalises*, Op. 85 (Milwaukee: G. Schirmer, Inc., 1967).

Appendix B: Working with Conductors

The relationship between singers and conductors is traditionally so unequal that I hesitate to offer comments to those on "the other side." Singers constantly face conductors, however, and they face us, so offering a deeper understanding of our inner life seems appropriate. We become accustomed to smiling and complying with them, but we rarely cross the line into genuine human contact, particularly if we are part of a group (a choir, a group of apprentices, or even a quartet of soloists). In talking with conductors about this book, at least one conductor has told me that he had never before thought about the inner life of a singer. Information usually lessens tension, and it seems that the singer/conductor relationship could become less adversarial with a more open dialogue.

Conductors so often seem to approach singers as though one or the other side is in charge and one of two balances of power must be determined immediately. Singers are either ants to be crushed by a heavy foot, or they are circus animals to be tamed with flattering words and a chair if necessary. In choirs, as well as alone, singers know when we frighten the conductors into embarrassed submission or hostile posturing. If the conductor comes from an instrumental rather than a vocal background, the chasm between him and his singers widens. As a singer, I do not pretend to understand the many facets of the conductor's ego. I do know that the emotional security of the maestro greatly affects my ability to sing without inhibition or distraction.

A singer friend recently told me about having asked the conductor of an opera company's young artists program why he spent so much time yelling at the apprentices. The maestro replied with astonishing honesty: "Everyone is insecure in this business. Yelling at you elevates me." In thinking about this exchange, I have wondered many things. Why does a man in the late prime of his career still feel insecure in front of a group of young apprentices? What does he hope to teach them by asserting his superiority over them when his position in relation to them is such an obvious fact? Does he get the musical result he seeks from behaving in this way, or are his feelings of inadequacy so strong that the musical process becomes secondary? What is he afraid will happen if he does not assert his authority?

The great African American leader Booker T. Washington once said, "There are two ways of exerting one's strength: one is pushing down, the other is pulling up."[1] Most conductors I have sung with choose one approach or the other, and the ones with whom I perform well generally choose to pull up the singers. In an argument with a conductor friend, I told him how much I had enjoyed working with a particular conductor who smiled before my entrances and made me feel welcome. My friend said, somewhat sarcastically, "So you want me to smile at you." Of course, my enjoyment of that experience was based in much more than a smile.

Personal Acceptance

A little bit of personal acceptance goes a long way when a singer stands in front of a conductor, especially if it's also in front of an orchestra. Conductors have a role similar to voice teachers in that they both balance the same two issues. The singer must know both that the conductor will have high standards and that he or she trusts in the singer's abilities. Singers are all too aware when a conductor has low expectations or lacks confidence in their talents. Nothing is worse for singers' mental and physical (i.e., vocal) state than feeling they must prove themselves to a conductor who has no faith in them. I find this to be equally true whether I am a soloist or a member of a large choir.

All musicians respond to gesture, of course, but something intangible happens to a singer's voice when following a conductor. It is nothing new to say that certain gestures affect our sound in specific ways. We also take on larger bodily characteristics of the conductor, which can have very positive or very negative effects on the physical functioning of our voices. Because rehearsal time is often short, we feel much of our personal acceptance by the conductor through nonverbal cues. The dynamic in the room always has an enormous impact on how freely our muscles will perform and with what emotional colors we will be able to infuse our voices. We draw quite a bit of vocal color from the emotional connection the conductor has with the music as well as from how he communicates his musical passion to us.

Conductors who aren't singers themselves may not understand that while all musicians must feel comfortable to play well, singers are even more profoundly affected by emotional attitudes because they literally *are* their own instruments. When a conductor singles out a singer for angry criticism, for example, that singer will feel a deep sense of personal shame. He or she was rejected by the maestro, not just his or her musical work. The conductors who achieve the most consistent musical results tend to be the ones who help everyone in the room do their best work. This may mean mixing humor and kindness with diligence during the rehearsals. In order for the conductor to be able to assess what is needed at any given moment, he must be able to focus on the other musicians without any distractions from worries about his own ego.

The Product vs. the Person

Understandably enough, many conductors become so concerned with the end product that they feel they don't have time to consider the emotional needs of the singers. I maintain that it doesn't take very much time to help the singers find a comfortable space. A few kind comments within a generally healthy approach to the project will be sufficient. The singers will be uncomfortable and tense if the conductor does not have a specific plan for rehearsals or seems overly worried about the success of the performance. (Nothing unnerves a singer faster than the feeling that no one is driving the bus.) If the conductor is secure enough to spend a few moments considering the human beings in front of him, he will instantly put the singers at ease. This time is well spent, as it will greatly improve the efficiency of the rehearsal as well as the commitment level of the singers during the final performance.

Some of the most frustrating situations for singers are productions in which they have been prepared by their regular choirmaster but are now conducted by someone else, either an opera conductor or an instrumental conductor. These primary conductors often have little understanding of what the singers need in terms of physical cues or emotional consideration. Too often, they also lack genuine respect for the choir's work and treat the choir as an inconvenient appendage. The singers of the choir can always sense immediately how each conductor feels about singers. Moreover, the members of the orchestra often reflect the attitude of the maestro.

A singer friend told me about another incident in which a guest conductor at an international opera house halted an orchestra rehearsal to berate the opera's chorus. The maestro ripped open his shirt, buttons flying, and told the chorus he wanted to see passion! "You're singing like a bunch of [inappropriate reference]!" Before the next chorus entrance, the choirmaster walked out onstage and raised an arm to silence his singers. "Maestro," he said, "you have two choices. Apologize to the chorus, or do this opera without one." The conductor apologized and continued the rehearsal, but he was never hired back by the company.

Recently I had an experience that was this incident's polar opposite. Graeme Jenkins, musical director of the Dallas Opera, came to the University of North Texas to conduct Handel's *Jephtha* in a joint concert with the Dallas Bach Society. Maestro Jenkins usually works with artists of international stature, yet he made the trip from Dallas to Denton quite often to prepare the North Texas students himself. Our students sang and played like they never had before. The maestro pushed them to new levels of emotional expression, inspiring them to perform this oratorio as an "opera during Lent." He held them to the highest standard, using humor along the way but never wasting time at rehearsals. Amazingly, he did all of this between rehearsals and performances of Verdi's *La traviata* at the Dallas Opera.

As the soprano soloist in the role of Jephtha's daughter (Iphis), I felt a great deal of pressure during the event. Maestro Jenkins coached me relentlessly but always kindly. I always felt that he was pushing me because I was capable of more, not because what I had offered was inadequate. This question of perspective is one I try to remember every day in my teaching and my singing. During these concerts, I did some of the most expressive, detailed singing of my life, because I wasn't afraid. The experience changed the way I approached all music from that moment on.

My most positive experiences with conductors have all been based in mutual respect. These gentlemen and women have been respectful of my time, patient with my physical illnesses when necessary, and kind as human beings, both on and off the podium. They don't attempt to "teach" me in front of the orchestra or speak to me in a condescending tone in any situation. They understand that as a singer, I need warmth and human acceptance from them to make my freest, most beautiful sounds. The singer/conductor relationship must be ego-free. The two sides don't have to know each other intimately, but they must accept one another and agree (usually in an unspoken way) to put the music first because it is bigger than either one of them individually.

Notes
1. Seldes, 724.

Closing Thoughts

In writing this book, I have spent a great deal of time thinking about what it means to have a healthy ego, to have real confidence rather than false conceit. As a singer, I think it comes down to having enough security in yourself to be able to focus entirely on what you are doing at the time. When we can focus, we are not distracted by irrelevant thoughts about what others are thinking of us, what we are thinking of our performance so far, what we had for lunch today, etc. It takes a great deal of personal confidence to tune out all of this chatter and stay with the music.

Recently, I watched the summer Olympic Games from Athens. Whenever I watch competitive Olympic sports, I am struck by the fact that at this stage all of the competitors are incredible athletes. The athletes who take home the gold medals are the ones who are able to focus, to block out the voices of the commentators and audience members, and simply do what they love, what they do best. Almost invariably, these are the athletes who, when interviewed, talk about trying to live up to their personal best. The ones who spoke before the competition about winning or outperforming the other athletes usually go home empty-handed.

The art of performance requires this type of concentration just as acutely, in part because it is an art form and not usually a direct competition between artists. The highest-level performing artists all share a remarkable ability to focus and live "in the moment," giving everything they have to their performances. It is much easier to talk about doing this than it is to do it.

I have realized that although I naturally have this sense of focus when I teach, I have to work much harder for it when I perform. While I am teaching in my studio, I am able to concentrate on the student, truly not thinking about anything but the task at hand. I have experienced this feeling, sometimes described by others as "being out of myself," when singing, but in many fewer circumstances. I think we all have to find the profession that takes us out of ourselves, and look for that feeling in the rest of our lives as well. When we are making a contribution to others and choosing not to focus on our own needs and desires, we are often surprised by the results.

As singers, we are fortunate to have this special way of expressing ourselves. We can use it to make art, to enrich our lives and the lives of others, or we can use it to push others out of our way in order to feel good about ourselves. We are all influenced by many people during our lives, from family members to friends to teachers to conductors, but, ultimately, we make our own choices about the kinds of artists we want to be. I hope that the experiences I have offered in these pages will lead you to new ways to cherish your own life as a singer.

Selected Resources

Armstrong, Lance. *It's Not About the Bike*. New York: Berkley Books, 2000.

Bennett-Goleman, Tara. *Emotional Alchemy: How the Mind Can Heal the Heart*. New York: Harmony Books, 2001.

Brown, Oren. *Discover Your Voice: How to Develop Healthy Voice Habits*. San Diego: Singular Publishing Group, 1996.

Bryan, Mark, with Julia Cameron and Catherine Allen. *The Artist's Way at Work: Riding the Dragon*. New York: William Morrow and Company, Inc., 1998.

Bunch, Meribeth. *Dynamics of the Singing Voice*. Wien, New York: Springer-Verlag, 1982.

Burns, David D. *The Feeling Good Handbook: Using the new mood therapy in everyday life*. New York: William Morrow, 1989.

Cameron, Julia. *The Artist's Way: A spiritual path to higher creativity*. New York: G.P. Putman's Sons, 1992.

___. *The Right to Write: An invitation and initiation into the writing life*. New York: Jeremy P. Tarcher/Putnam, 1998.

___. *The Vein of Gold: A journey to your creative heart*. New York: Putnam, 1996.

Casement, Patrick J. *Learning from the Patient*. Foreword by Robert S. Wallerstein. New York: Guilford Press, 1991.

Cather, Willa. *Song of the Lark*. New York: Penguin Books, 1991.

Chun-Tao Cheng, Stephen. *The Tao of Voice: A new East-West approach to transforming the singing and speaking voice*. Rochester, Vermont: Destiny Books, 1991.

Colijn, Helen. *Song of Survival*. Ashland, Oregon: White Cloud Press, 1995.

Corsini, Raymond J. and Alan J. Auerbach, editors. *Concise Encyclopedia of Psychology, Second Edition*. Abridged edition of the four-volume *Encyclopedia of Psychology, Second Edition*. New York: John Wiley & Sons, 1996.

Covey, Stephen R. *The Seven Habits of Highly Effective People*. New York: Simon and Schuster, 1989.

Csikzentmihalyi, Mihaly. *Creativity: Flow and the psychology of discovery and invention*. New York: HarperCollins Publishers, 1996.

__. *The Evolving Self: A Psychology for the Third Millennium*. New York: HarperCollins Publishers, 1993.

__. *Flow: The Psychology of Optimal Experience*. New York: Harper & Row, Publishers, 1990.

Dorneman, Joan, with Maria Caccia. *Complete Preparation: A guide to auditioning for opera*. Introduction by Sherrill and Nancy Milnes. New York: Excalibur Publishing, 1992.

Doscher, Barbara M. *The Functional Unity of the Singing Voice*. Metuchen, New Jersey: Scarecrow Press, 1994.

Emmons, Shirlee. *Power Performance for Singers: Transcending the barriers*. New York: Oxford University Press, 1998.

Frankl, Victor. *Man's Search for Meaning: An introduction to logotherapy*. Part one translated by Ilse Lasch. Preface by Gordon W. Allport. Fourth edition. Boston: Beacon Press, 1992.

Gardner, Howard. *Creating Minds: An anatomy of creativity seen through the lives of Freud, Einstein, Picasso, Stravinsky, Eliot, Graham, and Gandhi*. New York: Basic Books, 1993.

__. *Frames of Mind: The Theory of Multiple Intelligences*. New York: Basic Books, 1983.

Gawande, Atul. *Complications: A Surgeon's Notes on an Imperfect Science*. New York: Metropolitan Books, 2002.

Goldberg, Natalie. *Writing Down the Bones: Freeing the writer within*. Boston: Shambhala: Distributed by Random House, 1986.

Goleman, Daniel. *Emotional Intelligence*. New York: Bantam Books, 1995.

Gomes, Peter. *The Good Life: Truths that last in times of need*. New York: HarperSanFrancisco, 2002.

Green, Barry, with W. Timothy Gallwey. *The Inner Game of Music*. Garden City, New York: Anchor Press/Doubleday, 1986.

Hagen, Uta, with Haskel Frankel. *Respect for Acting*. New York: Macmillan Publishing Company, 1973.

Hahn, Reynaldo. *On Singers and Singing: Lectures and an Essay*. Translated by Léopold Simoneau. Introduction by Lorraine Gorrell. Discography by William R. Moran. Reinhard G. Pauly, general editor. First published by Editions Gallimard, 1957, as *Du Chant*. Portland, Oregon: Amadeus Press, 1990.

Hampton, Marion, editor, and Barbara Acker. *The Vocal Vision: Views on Voice by 24 Leading Teachers, Coaches, and Directors.* New York: Applause, 1997.

Hemsley, Thomas. *Singing and Imagination.* New York: Oxford University Press, 1998.

Hines, Jerome. *The Four Voices of Man.* New York: Limelight Editions, 1997.

__. *Great Singers on Great Singing.* New York: Limelight Editions, 1984.

Jordan, James. *The Musician's Soul.* Chicago: GIA Publications, Inc., 1998.

__. *The Musician's Spirit.* Chicago: GIA Publications, Inc., 2002.

Karas, Joza. *Music in Terezin.* New York: Beaufort Books, 1985.

Lamott, Anne. *Bird by Bird: Some Instructions on Writing and Life.* New York: Anchor Books, Doubleday, 1994.

Leonardi, Susan J., and Rebecca A. Pope. *The Diva's Mouth: Body, Voice, Prima Donna Politics.* New Brunswick, New Jersey: Rutgers University Press, 1996.

Linklater, Kristin. *Freeing the Natural Voice.* Drawings by Douglas Florian. New York: Drama Book Specialists, 1976.

Lloyd, Carol. *Creating a Life Worth Living: A practical course in career design for aspiring writers, artists, musicians, and others.* New York: HarperPerennial, 1997.

McKinney, James C. *The Diagnosis and Correction of Vocal Faults: A Manual for Teachers of Singing and for Choir Directors. Revised and expanded edition.* Nashville, Tennessee: Genevox Music Group, 1994.

Miller, Alice. *The Drama of the Gifted Child: The Search for the True Self.* Revised and updated with a new introduction by the author. Translated from the German by Ruth Ward. New York: Basic Books, 1994.

Miller, Arthur. *Death of a Salesman.* New York: Penguin Books, 1983. First published by The Viking Press, 1949.

Miller, Richard. *On the Art of Singing.* New York: Oxford University Press, 1996.

__. *The Structure of Singing: System and art in vocal technique.* New York: Schirmer Books, 1986.

Moore, Thomas. *Care of the Soul: A Guide for Cultivating Depth and Sacredness in Everyday Life*. New York: HarperPerennial, 1992.

Moriarty, John. *Diction*. Boston: E.C. Schirmer Music Company, 1975.

Palmer, Parker J. *The Courage to Teach: Exploring the Inner Landscape of a Teacher's Life*. San Francisco, California: Jossey-Bass, 1998.

Raessler, Kenneth R. *Aspiring to Excel*. Chicago: GIA Publications, Inc., 2004.

Ristad, Eloise. *A Soprano on Her Head: Right-side-up reflections on life and other performances*. Moab, Utah: Real People Press, 1982.

Russo, Richard. *Straight Man*. New York: Random House, Inc., 1997.

Sataloff, Robert Thayer, editor. *Professional Voice: The Science and Art of Clinical Care*. San Diego: Singular Publishing Group, 1997.

Sataloff, Robert Thayer and Deborah Caputo Rosen. *Psychology of Voice Disorders*. San Diego: Singular Publishing Group, 1997.

Sloan, Carolyn. *Finding Your Voice: A Practical and Spiritual Approach to Singing and Living*. New York: Hyperion, 1999.

Storr, Anthony. *Solitude: A Return to the Self*. New York: Ballantine Books, 1988.

Weisberger, Lauren. *The Devil Wears Prada*. New York: Doubleday, 2003.

Whitman, Walt. *Leaves of Grass*. Modern Library Edition. New York: Random House, 1993.

About the Author

Dr. Lynn Eustis is Assistant Professor of Voice at the University of North Texas. A native of Long Island, New York, she was previously Assistant Professor of Voice/Opera at Howard Payne University. Eustis earned a Bachelor of Music from Bucknell University, a Master of Music from the Curtis Institute of Music, and a Doctor of Music in Opera from Florida State University.

Eustis can be heard annually as a recital soloist at the Hudebni Festival Vysocina in the Czech Republic. She has appeared at the Brevard Music Center, the National Opera Company, the Ash Lawn-Highland Festival, and the European Opera Center in Belgium. Roles performed include the title role in *Lucia di Lammermoor*, Rosina in *The Barber of Seville*, Marie in *The Daughter of the Regiment*, Pamina in *The Magic Flute*, and Susanna in *The Marriage of Figaro*.

Eustis appears regularly as a soloist with such organizations as the Dallas Bach Society, Fort Worth Dallas Ballet, the Atlanta Baroque Orchestra, the Dallas Symphony Orchestra, the San Angelo Symphony, Fort Worth Early Music, the Orchestra of New Spain, and Concert Royal in New York City. She is a frequent lecturer on music of the Holocaust, including presentations at the College Music Society annual meeting in Denver, the Texoma Region NATS Artist Series, and the TMEA Convention.